First World War
and Army of Occupation
War Diary
France, Belgium and Germany

28 DIVISION
Divisional Troops
146 Brigade Royal Field Artillery
22 December 1914 - 18 October 1915

WO95/2271/6

The Naval & Military Press Ltd
www.nmarchive.com
Published in association with The National Archives

Published by

The Naval & Military Press Ltd

Unit 10 Ridgewood Industrial Park,

Uckfield, East Sussex,

TN22 5QE England

Tel: +44 (0) 1825 749494

www.naval-military-press.com

www.nmarchive.com

This diary has been reprinted in facsimile from the original. Any imperfections are inevitably reproduced and the quality may fall short of modern type and cartographic standards.

© **Crown Copyright**
Images reproduced by permission of The National Archives, London, England, 2015.

Contents

Document type	Place/Title	Date From	Date To
Miscellaneous	WO95/2271/6		
Heading	28th Division Divl Artillery 146th Brigde R. F. A. Dec 1914-Oct 1915		
Heading	28th Division 146th Bde R. F. A. Vol I 22.12.14-28.1.15		
War Diary	Winchester	22/12/1914	05/01/1915
War Diary	Kings Worthy	05/01/1915	19/01/1915
War Diary	Le Havre	20/01/1915	20/01/1915
War Diary	Cassel	21/01/1915	21/01/1915
War Diary	Hazebrouck	22/01/1915	22/01/1915
War Diary	Near Caestre	23/01/1915	31/01/1915
Heading	28th Division 146th Bde. R.F.A. Vol II 1-28-2.15		
War Diary	Ypres	01/02/1915	28/02/1915
Heading	146th Bde R.F.A. Vol III 28th Division 1-31.3.15		
War Diary	Ypres	01/03/1915	31/03/1915
Heading	28th Division 146th Bde R.F.A. Vol IV 1.4-30/4/15		
War Diary	Ypres	01/04/1915	13/04/1915
War Diary	Zonnebeke	14/04/1915	30/04/1915
Heading	Nr Cadery		
Miscellaneous	Priors Barton Winchester. Winchester 615 Original returned 17/4/25	16/04/1915	16/04/1915
Miscellaneous	CXLVI Bde R.F.A. 28th Division	21/11/1915	21/11/1915
Miscellaneous	From Colonel G.R.T. Rundle. C.B. Re 2nd Ypres.	21/11/1925	21/11/1925
Miscellaneous	Priors Barton Winchester	16/04/1925	16/04/1925
War Diary	149th Battery R.F.A.	22/04/1915	05/05/1915
Heading	28th Division 146th Brigade R.F.A. Vol V 1st-30.5.15		
War Diary		01/05/1915	01/05/1915
War Diary	Zonnebeke	02/05/1915	03/05/1915
War Diary	Poperinghe	04/05/1915	22/05/1915
War Diary	Ypres	24/04/1915	30/04/1915
Heading	28th Division 146th Bde R.F.A. Vol VI 31.5-30.6.15		
War Diary	Nr Winnezeele	31/05/1915	17/06/1915
War Diary	Dickebusch	18/06/1915	30/06/1915
Heading	28th Division 146th Bde R.F.A. Vol VII		
War Diary		01/07/1915	17/07/1915
War Diary	Dranoutre	17/07/1915	30/07/1915
Heading	28th Division 146th Bde R.F.A. Vol VIII August 15		
War Diary		31/07/1915	31/08/1915
Heading	28th Division 146th Bde R.F.A. Vol IX Sept 15		
War Diary		01/09/1915	26/09/1915
War Diary	Bethune	29/09/1915	01/10/1915
Heading	28th Division 146th Bde R.F.A. Vol X Oct 15		
War Diary	Cambrin	02/10/1915	31/10/1915
Miscellaneous	A Form. Messages And Signals.		
Miscellaneous	BM 478	30/09/1915	30/09/1915
Operation(al) Order(s)	28th Divisional Artillery Operation Order No 47	28/09/1915	28/09/1915
Miscellaneous	Progress Report 149 Battery R.F.A.	02/10/1915	02/10/1915
War Diary	O.C. 146 Bde	04/10/1915	04/10/1915
War Diary	28th Divl Arty O.O. No 50	03/10/1915	03/10/1915
Miscellaneous	BM 495	02/10/1915	02/10/1915

Miscellaneous		01/10/1915	01/10/1915
Miscellaneous	C Form (Original). Messages And Signals.	01/09/1915	01/09/1915
Miscellaneous	28th Divisional Artillery Operation Order No. 41	19/09/1915	19/09/1915
Miscellaneous	Table Showing Positions to be taken over by 28th Divisional Artillery		
Miscellaneous	Amendment to Tables of Rates and Distribution of Fire.	12/10/1915	12/10/1915
Miscellaneous	Amendments to Operation Order No. 51	10/10/1915	10/10/1915
Miscellaneous	28th Divisional Artillery Operation Order No. 51	09/10/1915	09/10/1915
Miscellaneous	Distribution Of Fire Of 28th Divisional Artillery		
Miscellaneous	28th Divisional Artillery. Addition to Operation Order No 51 dated 9th October 1915.	11/10/1915	11/10/1915
Miscellaneous	146 Bde	11/10/1915	11/10/1915
War Diary	28th Divisional Artillery Operation Order No. 52	16/10/1915	16/10/1915
War Diary	Programme of the distribution of fire to support the Bombing attack of the Guards Brigades		
War Diary	28th Divisional Artillery Operation Order No. 53	18/10/1915	18/10/1915

WO95/2271/6

28TH DIVISION
DIVL ARTILLERY

146TH BRIGDE R.F.A.
DEC 1914 - OCT 1915

2. gr. Division

146ter Bde R.I.R.

121/4193

Vol I. 22.12.14 — 28.1.15.

Army Form C. 2118.

WAR DIARY
or
INTELLIGENCE SUMMARY.
(Erase heading not required.)

Instructions regarding War Diaries and Intelligence Summaries are contained in F.S. Regs., Part II. and the Staff Manual respectively. Title pages will be prepared in manuscript.

Hour, Date, Place	Summary of Events and Information	Remarks and references to Appendices
WINCHESTER.		
22nd December 1914.	146 Brigade R.F.A. formed. (Major T.E.P. Wickham temporarily in command.) forming part of 28th Division Batteries. 75th from 3rd Bde R.F.A 366th which was left half Battery of 62nd Battery R.F.A from 3rd Bde R.F.A 367th which was left half of 75th Bty R.F.A	
Dec. 23rd To Dec. 31st.	Brigade forming and mobilising in billets. Bt Col. F.J.S. Cleeve commanded from 27/12/14	585.
1st January 1915.	4/1/15.	
Jan. 2nd	366th Bty. moved into billets at Martyr Worthy.	585.
Jan 3rd	75th Bty. moved into billets at Itchen Abbas. Bde. H.Q.S. moved into billets at Kingsworthy. 367th Bty moved into billets at Headburn Worthy. 146 Bde. Am. Col. moved into billets at Kingsworthy and Headburn Worthy.	585. 185.
Jan 5th	Bt. Col. G.R.T. Rundle assumed command of 146 Bde	185.

WAR DIARY
or
INTELLIGENCE SUMMARY.
(Erase heading not required.)

Army Form C. 2118.

Hour, Date, Place	Summary of Events and Information	Remarks and references to Appendices
KINGS WORTHY. JAN. 6th to 14th 1915.	Brigade mobilising. Officers of Brigade. Head quarters. B? Col. G. R.T. RUNDLE Lieut & Adjutant S.D. GRAHAM. M.O. Lieut D. McVICKER R.A.M.C. V.O. Lieut T.M. MICHELL A.V.C. (SR). 75th Battery R.F.A. Major. N.G.M. JERVIS. 2/Lieut. E.H. COAD. 2/Lieut. P.M.O.F. HOSACK. 2/Lieut. G.R. RENNY. 367th Battery R.F.A. Capt. B.V. MACDONAGH. Lieut. G. TUITE-DALTON. Lieut. F. JOHNSTONE. Lieut. E.J. STANSFIELD. 366th Battery RFA. Major. T.E.P. WICKHAM. Lieut. C.R.F. HAY-WEBB 2/Lieut. H.J. COOLEY. 2/Lieut. W.E. BALCOMBE-BROWN. 146 Bde. Ammn Col. Capt. C.W. HINCE. 2/Lieut. E.G. STOYLE. Lieut. G.C. RUSSELL Lieut. E.F. HAYES.	
JAN. 13th	H.M. KING GEORGE V. inspected 28th Division on FAWLEY DOWN. WINCHESTER.	SEE
JAN. 15th 12.33 p.m.	Lieut COOLEY and 2 men per Battery and Column sent on ahead to arrange billets in FRANCE.	SEE

Army Form C. 2118.

WAR DIARY
or
INTELLIGENCE SUMMARY.
(Erase heading not required.)

Instructions regarding War Diaries and Intelligence Summaries are contained in F.S. Regs., Part II. and the Staff Manual respectively. Title pages will be prepared in manuscript.

Hour, Date, Place	Summary of Events and Information	Remarks and references to Appendices
KINGSWORTHY. JAN. 16TH 1915.	Mobilization of the Brigade almost complete. Orders received to march to SOUTHAMPTON. JAN 17TH 1915.	S&T
10 pm	Orders for march cancelled.	
JAN. 17TH. 7 pm	Orders received to march to SOUTHAMPTON. JAN. 18TH 1915.	S&T
JAN. 18TH.	Marched to SOUTHAMPTON in following order from starting Point 1 mile North of COMPTON. Fine sunny day	
	146TH BDE. AMM TN COL. 8.55 A.M.	
	75TH BTY. RFA ---- 9.10 A.M.	
	367 BTY. RFA ---- 9.20 A.M.	
	366 BTY RFA ---- 9.30 A.M.	
	146TH BDE H.Qs ---- 9.45 A.M.	
	Route. na. TWYFORD-ALLBROOK-EASTLEIGH-SOUTHAMPTON.	
	Entrained at SOUTHAMPTON DOCKS as under.	
	HQs and 367TH BTY. RFA on S.S. MATHERAN. sailed 5 p.m.	
	75TH BTY. RFA. on S.S. ATLANTIAN. " 6 p.m.	
	366TH BTY & 146 BDE. A.C. on S.S. ARCHITECT. " 6 p.m.	
JAN. 19TH. 10 am	Arrived at LE HAVRE after very calm passage, and unloaded in the docks. Warm clothing drawn.	S&T
6 pm	75TH BTY marched to GARE DES MARCHANDISES, LE HAVRE. and entrained	

Army Form C. 2118.

WAR DIARY
or
INTELLIGENCE SUMMARY.
(Erase heading not required.)

Instructions regarding War Diaries and Intelligence Summaries are contained in F.S. Regs., Part II. and the Staff Manual respectively. Title pages will be prepared in manuscript.

Hour, Date, Place	Summary of Events and Information	Remarks and references to Appendices
JAN. 20TH. 6.30am	H.Q.s and 367TH BTY. entrained at GARE. DES MARCHANDISES	
LE HAVRE. 10.30am.	and started.	
2.30pm	146.BDE.A.C. entrained and started from GARE DES MARCHANDISES.	S85
10.30pm	366 BTY RFA " " " " " "	
11.pm	75TH BTY arrived at HAZEBROUCK detrained marched to billets	
	1 MILE S.W. of CAESTRE.	
JAN. 21ST. CASSEL	HQs & 367TH BTY detrained and marched to billets 1 MILE.	S85
7am to 9.45 am	S.W of CAESTRE. arriving 3p.m.	
HAZEBROUCK. 10pm	366 Bty. RFA arrived, remained the night time	
	146. BDE. Am. Col. arrived at HAZEBROUCK detrained marched	
	to billets with rest of BDE.	
JAN. 22nd.	Brigade remained in billets and opened u/s.	S85
Near CAESTRE		S85
Jan 23rd to 31st	Brigade Training in billets	
Jan 26TH 27TH	Bde on Emergency duty. Sir Jn. French C in C	S85
28TH	Bde inspected by Gen. French C in C	

(73989) W4141—163. 400,000. 9/14. H.&J.Ltd. Forms/C. 2118/10.

28th Division

121/4505

146th Bde: R.F.A.

Vol II. 1 – 28.2.15

WAR DIARY or INTELLIGENCE SUMMARY.

(Erase heading not required.)

Army Form C. 2118.

51

Hour, Date, Place	Summary of Events and Information	Remarks and references to Appendices
YPRES. FEBRUARY 1st 7.20am. 6.20pm Feb 2nd 1.am. 9am 7.20am 5.20am	Bde Hqs and Right battery of each battery and half the Amm. Col. marched to VLAMERTINGHE and encamped one mile S.W of VLAMERTINGHE. 4.30 pm. The Bde Hq. Signallers and the Firing Battery of the above Sections marched through YPRES and came into action as under relieving sections of French Artillery (9th Regt). Bde Hqs at Chateau on Mile E by S of YPRES Ref. Map. BELGIUM B Series. Sheet 28.N.W. Sq. I.15.d.99. 75E Bty on Rly. Sq. I.15.B.1.4. 367E " just N of Rly. Sq. I.15.B.8.6. 366E - Sq. I.11.D.10.2. Horses and gun limbers returned Knapu line. Sections ready to open fire, lines laid out. Concealed from aircraft. Gunners in dug outs prepared by the French that we relieved - Telephonic communication established with C.R.A. Sections Registered their Zones - Left half Battery marched to VLAMERTINGHE arriving 2.30pm Left half Btys marched to their position in action as above. But did not come into action as the French Sections	SOS

Army Form C. 2118.

6

WAR DIARY
or
INTELLIGENCE SUMMARY.
(Erase heading not required.)

Instructions regarding War Diaries and Intelligence Summaries are contained in F.S. Regs., Part II and the Staff Manual respectively. Title pages will be prepared in manuscript.

Hour, Date, Place	Summary of Events and Information	Remarks and references to Appendices
Continued FEB 2nd	did not leave that night owing to news received that the Germans intended to attack in force. Nothing of note happened during the night. The French Batteries who relieved ours they had been in the position for over a month and had not had one single casualty among the men.	S.E.C.
FEB 3rd	Trouble with telephone wires being cut repeatedly. Batteries fired a few rounds each at German trenches at ZWARTELEEN and Point 60 Sq. 129 C 91. French Sections departed 5 p.m. Our Sections joined in their emplacements. German aeroplanes active during the day. Concealment from them all important.	Ref. Map. BELGIUM "B" Series Sheet 28 N.W. 1/20000
FEB 4th 10 am	75th & 367th Batteries shelled VERBRANDEN MOLEN – HOLLEBEKE Road and ZWARTELEEN – KLEIN ZILLEBEKE Road respectively. Infantry reported the fire very effective. 51 rds fired altogether. German aeroplanes very active during the afternoon.	
9.30 pm	News received from C.R.A. that 83rd Inf by Bde were going to attack German trenches in woods in Sq. I 34. C. 3rd Bdn R.F.A. reported they were supporting by firing on point I 34.d. 6.0. and road running S.W. from it. also ridge over canal at Point O.5.B.85.	S.E.C.

WAR DIARY
or
INTELLIGENCE SUMMARY.
(Erase heading not required.)

Army Form C. 2118.

7

Hour, Date, Place	Summary of Events and Information	Remarks and references to Appendices
YPRES FEB 4th 10 pm.	Fire opened by all three batteries on three points. Aim and range obtained from the map: delay in firing due to the fact that no information had been given us of the position of our trenches or the enemy's except in our own immediate zone. And except information given us by the French C.O. that we relieved, no information has been given us of position of German batteries while we have been here —	
10.30 pm	Batteries ceased fire under orders from C.R.A. 1st 31st Bde having got onto the above points. French 9th Corps dug emplacements not in the open 200 yds to the N.E. of E of 367th Bty. This was observed by aircraft & shelled — This also drew attention to our positions. 75th fired 180 - 367 - 27 rds. and 366 Bty 72 rds. — The 366th Bty also fired on Point 60. In the morning the Pt.e Vaf. Bde asked us to fire on any buildings occupied by the Germans in our zone — we were unable to do so having no High Explosive shell —	SES

WAR DIARY
or
INTELLIGENCE SUMMARY.
(Erase heading not required.)

Army Form C. 2118.

Hour, Date, Place	Summary of Events and Information	Remarks and references to Appendices
FEB 6th 1 am	366 E Bty reported that they had turned out with rifles as there was heavy firing on their left. Caused by a house containing a reserve of ammunition having caught on fire – hot being needed they returned after about one hour – 32 rds of H.E. shell brought up by 146 Bde Amn Col. 9 given to 367th 175th Battery. Nothing much done during the day. We were asked by the infantry to fire on Germans and search and sweep on Sq. I 35 & 34 d. All three batteries fired. 272 rds fired.	
6.40 pm	Under secret instructions from C.R.A. fire opened on German supports in our own zone - to keep them from reinforcing their line while the P3rd Inf. Bde attacked them in the night I am zone. The main trench till 9.40 pm. 186 rds fire. Reported it be very effective, so much so that the K.O.Y.L.I. against their trenches and were enabled to lie on	
9.30 pm	top of their parapets and fire –	S.K.G.

Army Form C. 2118.

9.

WAR DIARY
or
INTELLIGENCE SUMMARY.
(Erase heading not required.)

Instructions regarding War Diaries and Intelligence Summaries are contained in F.S. Regs., Part II. and the Staff Manual respectively. Title pages will be prepared in manuscript.

Hour, Date, Place	Summary of Events and Information	Remarks and references to Appendices
YPRES. Feb 6th 5.20 p.m.	Batteries registered only - 367th Bty fired 6 rds on German machine gun in Sq I 35 A 99	SDG R.P.
Feb 13 7th	A quiet day. Capt. R. Parbury joined the Brigade and posted as adjutant.	R.P.
FEB. 8th	367th Battery registered only.	R.P.
FEB. 9th		
2 p.m.	75th Battery commenced registering. About an hour later 367th Battery registered.	R.P.
FEB 10th 8 a.m.	"75th" Battery was under enemy's shell fire (H.E.) for half an hour - rate of enemy fire slow. No damage done.	
12. Midnight	367th Battery shelled from the S.E. and again at 3 a.m. next morning.	R.P.
FEB 11th 4.15 p.m.	367th Battery registered.	
5.55 p.m.	367. Battery opened fire on enemy's gun.	

(73389) W4141—463. 400,000. 9/14. H.&J.Ltd. Forms/C. 2118/10.

Army Form C. 2118.

10

WAR DIARY
or
INTELLIGENCE SUMMARY.
(Erase heading not required.)

Instructions regarding War Diaries and Intelligence Summaries are contained in F.S. Regs., Part II. and the Staff Manual respectively. Title pages will be prepared in manuscript.

Hour, Date, Place	Summary of Events and Information	Remarks and references to Appendices
YPRES. FEB 11th 5.55 p.m.	near KLEIN ZILLEBEKE which had been shelling our cavalry in their trenches. We also asked a French Battery on our left to assist but they did not open fire. The 367th Battery fired 20 rounds —	K.P.
FEB 12th	The 367th Battery opened fire on two German lorries at a range of 3500 in Square J.25.d (Belgium sheet 28 N.W. 1/20000) at the request of G.O.C. 83rd Inf. Bde. No direct observation was obtainable and the result was therefore unknown.	K.P.
FEB 13th	Registering only —	K.P.
FEB 14th 3 p.m.	Registered. Heavy gun and rifle fire on our right. This appears to have been an attack to regain a trench lost lying	C.S.
FEB 15th 3.30 a.m.	Received following message from F.O.O. R.A. 80 (verbal.) "Own attack last night failed to Kl. h sway 65228.	

(73989) W4141—463. 400,000. 9/14. H.&J.Ltd. Forms/C. 2118/10.

Army Form C. 2118.

WAR DIARY
or
INTELLIGENCE SUMMARY.
(Erase heading not required.)

Instructions regarding War Diaries and Intelligence Summaries are contained in F. S. Regs., Part II. and the Staff Manual respectively. Title pages will be prepared in manuscript.

Hour, Date, Place	Summary of Events and Information	Remarks and references to Appendices
YPRES. FEB 15th 3.30 a.m. 4.26 a.m.	You will open fire with all your guns at dawn. each gun to fire in its own zone. The Batteries opened fire. Not long afterwards the stunning officer reported all quiet on front and the fire was stopped by order by the C.R.A.	R.P.
FEB. 16th 2 a.m.	The observation officers reported that our infantry expected to be attacked at dawn. But nothing happened and the rest of the day was quiet.	
9 p.m.	Heavy rifle fire broke out in front. The Rain Battalion at once turned jit to be taking place in the cellos to the right of our Zone.	R.P.
9.10 p.m.	Battery ceased fire.	
FEB 17th	During the night some 30m bombs in the middle of our zone were thrown in by the enemy and occupied by him.	
8.15 a.m.	The O.C. left infantry brigade regretted as to fire on the enemy's supports at the same time informing us that a counter attack against the position not trenches was being organised and would take place in about 3/4 hours time.	R.P.

Army Form C. 2118.

/2.

WAR DIARY
or
INTELLIGENCE SUMMARY.
(Erase heading not required.)

Hour, Date, Place	Summary of Events and Information	Remarks and references to Appendices
YPRES. FEB. 19th	This counter attack was eventually made and failed in its object. This Brigade was not informed when the attack took place.	During this fighting considerable trouble was experienced with the telephone communications. The wires were continually being cut. The wire issued to Brigades is neither strong enough nor sufficient in quantity for this kind of siege warfare. Without reliable telephone communications it is impossible for the artillery to give the effective support to the infantry and its units is of such vital importance —
9.30 a.m.	The Mill battery in conjunction with No. 101 or Belgian battery and a French 75-m.m battery heavily bombarded the enemy's trenches and supports while another attack by our infantry was organised. This attack was eventually successful and the trench regained.	
2.15 p.m.	The 75th battery received to try H.E. German shells very close to their position.	
6.40 p.m.	It was reported from 83rd Inf. Bde. that the Germans were advancing behind Hill 60. The Battery (ys. 367) searched behind the hill for about 1 hour. It was afterwards that these men seen were those who had been shewn out of their trenches on Hill 60 and the battery stopped firing.	
FEB. 18th	A quiet day.	R.a.m.c.
FEB. 19th	A quiet day. Lieut. A. Kenan Taylor joined the Bde. Vice Lieut. McVickers R.a.m.c.	K.P.

Army Form C. 2118.

13.

WAR DIARY
or
INTELLIGENCE SUMMARY.
(Erase heading not required.)

Instructions regarding War Diaries and Intelligence Summaries are contained in F.S. Regs., Part II. and the Staff Manual respectively. Title pages will be prepared in manuscript.

Hour, Date, Place	Summary of Events and Information	Remarks and references to Appendices
YPRES FEB 20th	A quiet day.	
8.15 p.m.	Following message received from B.M. R.A. "The Infantry Brigade holding the left section will be relieved about 9 p.m. this evening by Nineteenth Infantry Brigade. A.A.A. All guns to be ready to open fire on their own zones if required. A.A.A. Intimate touch must be kept up with Infantry Brigade Commander in your own section. A.A.A. Acknowledge. B.M. R.A. 4.25 P.M.	K?
FEB 21st	Very quiet day.	
7.55 p.m.	Message received as follows :— "The relief of the 84th Infantry Brigade by the 9th I. Brigade is to be carried out tonight commencing at 8 p.m. & continuing probably to a late hour. J.a. B.M. Commanders will keep close touch with the Infy. Commanders in their sections, and will be ready to establish the fire de barrage in their own zones at short notice. This is especially important in the case of the 3rd Bde. Q and A Belgian Batteries. The 37th Btty should be prepared to open on the German Main Guard S.W. of Canal bow O. if required" B.M. R.A.	K?
7.10 P.M.	The batteries were not required to open fire.	

Army Form C. 2118.

WAR DIARY
or
INTELLIGENCE SUMMARY.
(Erase heading not required.)

Hour, Date, Place	Summary of Events and Information	Remarks and references to Appendices
YPRES FEB 22nd	Received following message :- B.M. 71.	
4.45. p.m.	"Enemy mortar just in rear of his trench I.29.d.3.c.8 now shelling our trenches aaa Please turn on your guns if possible AAA." from 13th Inf. Bde. 4.35 p.m. The 76th Battery at once opened fire and silenced the mortar about the 4th shot.	
6.40 p.m.	Message from 13th Inf. Bde :- B.m. 76. "ZWARTELEEN Salient has been severely bombed and trench damaged AAA. Our firing line has been reinforced in view of a possible attack by enemy. AAA. Be prepared to assist." 6.40 p.m. The batteries stood ready but no attack was made.	K.P.
FEB 23rd 2.5 p.m.	Message from 13th Inf Bde :- (B.M. 96) "The trenches 46, 47, 48 are being shelled by light field gun from direction of ZWARTELEEN wood probably X rds at SE corner of I.35.a. Please assist." Fire was at once opened.	
3.40 p.m.	Message from 13 Inf Bde :- B.M. 98. "Enemies guns still firing over ZWARTELEEN from S.S.E." Fire was reopened on this area.	K.P.

WAR DIARY
or
INTELLIGENCE SUMMARY.
(Erase heading not required.)

Army Form C. 2118.

/5.

Hour, Date, Place	Summary of Events and Information	Remarks and references to Appendices
YPRES. FEB 24th 8.30 p.m.	367 :- 75 Battery opened fire on enemy mortar.	
10.15 am.	Message from 13 Inf Bde. B.M.112:- "Trench mortars has been started firing."	
10.33 am	Report from 13 Inf.Bde to open fire again on mortar. This was done.	
10.45 am	Message from 13th Inf Bde. P.m 1114:- "HE how falling near 46 trench M.M. Cannot give direction which they come from. Suggest generally trenches between ZWARTELEEN and railway and railway cutting. MM also opposite 36 & 37 west of railway cutting. MM also opposite 31 Bde." refuted 116 Bde.	
10.50 am	Message from 13th Inf. Bde. B.M. 115":- Shell S.E. of ZWARTELEEN also opposite 38 A.A.A."	
12.28 p.m.	Message from 13th Bde: "Enemy light field gun now firing from S.S.E of ZWARTELEEN enfilading 46 trench."	
12.48 p.m.	Report to entered capital from 13th Inf Bde. On receipt of these messages fire was opened at once on every occasion.	R.P.

WAR DIARY
or
INTELLIGENCE/SUMMARY.
(Erase heading not required.)

Army Form C. 2118.

16

Hour, Date, Place	Summary of Events and Information	Remarks and references to Appendices
YPRES. FEB 24th.	The 367th and 75th Batteries kept up the fire till about 5.30 p.m. when firing ceased.	R.P.
FEB 25th	During the morning and afternoon the 13th Inft. Bde. requested the fire of the guns to be directed onto enemy's light field gun which was shelling our trenches on the left of the line - firing was kept up at intervals by the 366 and 367 Batteries. The infantry reported the fire was well directed.	
3.0 p.m.	Received a verbal message from the OC.R.A. to state firing - This was to find out which batteries were shelling their trenches. This was subsequently found to be enemy own fire.	
	Received verbal message from B.M. R.A. to effect that a prisoner had reported to 13th Inft. Bde. that enemy intended to attack our trenches in Sector C. at 12 midnight.	
12 midnight.	This report proved to be unreliable and no attack was made.	R.P.

Army Form C. 2118.

17

WAR DIARY
or
INTELLIGENCE SUMMARY.
(Erase heading not required.)

Hour, Date, Place		Summary of Events and Information	Remarks and references to Appendices
YPRES.	FEB. 26th 1.16 p.m.	Received message from 13 Inf Bde:- (BM 184) "Short-range from left of KLEIN ZILLEBEKE reported by D sector." The 75th Battery swept and searched east of KLEIN ZILLEBEKE.	
	2.0 p.m.	Message from 13 Inf Bde:- "Enemy shelling of trenches ceased."	
	8.30 p.m.	The 83rd Inf Bde returned the 15th K Bde in the K.P. Trenches.	
	FEB. 27th	The 367th Battery fired on enemy trench mortar turn in their trenches. The fire was effective.	
	FEB. 28th	A quiet day.	

146th Bde. R.F.A.

Vol III 1 - 31.3.15

28th Division

Army Form C. 2118.

18

WAR DIARY
or
INTELLIGENCE SUMMARY.
(Erase heading not required.)

Instructions regarding War Diaries and Intelligence Summaries are contained in F.S. Regs., Part II. and the Staff Manual respectively. Title pages will be prepared in manuscript.

Hour, Date, Place	Summary of Events and Information	Remarks and references to Appendices
1915. YPRES. March 1st	A quiet day. The Brigade came under the orders of Col: Duffus R.F.A. commanding the Left group.	N.P.
" 2nd	75th Battery fired two series on enemy light field guns which were shelling our trenches.	K.P.
" 3rd	The 366 and 367 Batteries fired about 4 salvos each on enemy trenches. The Infantry reported that the two fires went right into the enemy trenches.	
11 a.m.	In the afternoon the 366 Battery were heavily shelled from the S.E. and had one gun wheel & one limber wheel broken.	K.P.
" 4th	The three batteries turned their fire onto the enemy trenches to their own zones. firing 4 or 5 salvos.	K.P.
11.40 a.m.		
12.10 p.m.	The 75th Battery fired on enemy left field gun in square I 35 A.	K.P.

Army Form C. 2118.

19.

WAR DIARY
or
INTELLIGENCE/SUMMARY.
(Erase heading not required.)

Instructions regarding War Diaries and Intelligence
Summaries are contained in F.S. Regs., Part II
and the Staff Manual respectively. Title pages
will be prepared in manuscript.

Hour, Date, Place	Summary of Events and Information	Remarks and references to Appendices
YPRES. March 5th		
9.5. a.m.	The three batteries opened fire on enemy field guns on order from Left Group Commander. "Short range". 75th Battery opened. I.36.c. 367. I.36.d. 366. J.31.d.	"Short Range" and "Shell" are code words sent back by the infantry. The former means Fat ur trenches are being bombarded by light & field guns. The latter means Fat they are being shelled by K.P. Trench mortar n minnenwerfer
{ 11.45 a.m. 12.10 p.m.	The 75's and 367th Batteries opened fire in response to the message "Short range".	
	Up to 6 p.m. these two batteries on their further occasions fired on receipt of this message "Short range".	
	The 149 Batty (late 92 Ltd) came under the orders of O.C. 146 Bde.	Officers of 149 Batty. Capt. R.G. Ellis Lt. Jann Lt. Coles 2Lt. Russell
March 6.	367th Battery fired on guns in O.6.C.22 on message "Short range" from observing station	
10.30 a.m.	"Short Range". 367th Battery opened fire in I.36.C. 75th Battery on I.36.C.	K.P.
1.40 p.m.	In the evening a wire was laid out to trench 39. The 366 Battery were connected up with trench 46.	K.P.

WAR DIARY
or
INTELLIGENCE SUMMARY.
(Erase heading not required.)

Army Form C. 2118.

20

Hour, Date, Place	Summary of Events and Information	Remarks and references to Appendices
YPRES March 7.	?hiding	
2.5. p.m.	The west [Yorks] sent in "Short-Range message": "Thought left group commander - 367 + 75 Batteries shelled enemy trenches.	
March 8th		
7. a.m.	"Short range message" dual group trenches. 367 Btty. fired at guns in O.B.a. 75th Battery fired in ZWARTELEEN.	
	"Short Range message" left group Batteries. 75 and 366 Batteries fired on German trenches - 367 fired on guns in I.36.d.4.8.	
10.40 a.m.	"Short Range" message. All trees + trees retaliated on German trenches.	
10.45 a.m.	367th Battery sent letter into info re new KLEIN ZILLEBEKE on information from informer.	
10.52 a.m.	75th Battery received msg from 361 C25 on receipt of further information from our own left battery. O.P.	

Instructions regarding War Diaries and Intelligence
Summaries are contained in F.S. Regs., Part II.
and the Staff Manual respectively. Title pages
will be prepared in manuscript.

WAR DIARY
or
INTELLIGENCE SUMMARY.
(Erase heading not required.)

Army Form C. 2118.

21.

Hour, Date, Place	Summary of Events and Information	Remarks and references to Appendices
YPRES. March 8th. 11 a.m.	All of following found on men seen out to German trenches:—	
11.30 a.m.	Received order to "stop firing from B.O.S." This apparently is to find out which brigade was firing shot.	R.O.
2.15 p.m.	2/D. Brig. of Huzzars were billetted by heavy howitzer fire yesterday. They had not been permitted to move. Actual damage done was spiteful.	P.O.
	"Our B.L. 6" nose fuzed —"	
March 9th. 12.30 am	Received message from Left Group Commander — "An enemy mine has been exploded close up to H.9 trench. The R.E. officer on the spot thinks that it is in an advanced stage, and that it will probably be exploded within tonight's tomorrow night. Please arrange to have as many guns as possible laid on the spot to fire as close to the trenches as is compatible with safety to deal with hostile supports etc. coming up. Also please be ready to open fire instantly if called upon but do not open fire unless called upon by 13 Inf. Bde. Bn H.Q. Left Group Commander N. trenches about 40 yards hostile trench are very close at this point."	R.O.

Army Form C. 2118.

22

WAR DIARY
or
INTELLIGENCE SUMMARY
(Erase heading not required.)

Instructions regarding War Diaries and Intelligence Summaries are contained in F.S. Regs., Part II and the Staff Manual respectively. Title pages will be prepared in manuscript.

Hour, Date, Place	Summary of Events and Information	Remarks and references to Appendices
YPRES. March 9th		
10.47 a.m.	If called upon to fire rounds do not spare ammunition. All three batteries were at once laid on this point. 367th & 75th batteries fired on German trenches in front of our trenches 36 & 37. 366th Battery fired on guns in P.1 a 21.	
1.30 p.m.	367 & 75th Battery fired 2 salvos each on German trenches	
1.40 p.m.	367 & 75th Battery fired 1 salvo each on same trenches while 366 Battery fired on guns in P.7 a 7.9. The above programme was in accordance with instructions previously received from the left group leader.	
3.5-7 p.m.	"Short range" message from left Bn. H.Q. The 367th fired two salvos on German trenches.	
8	During the afternoon Major T.M.S.P. Wickham D.S.O. commanding 366 Battery was wounded whilst near his observation station. He was removed to hospital the same night.	R.P.
March 10th		
12.3 p.m.	In accordance with daily programme the 367 & 366 Batteries fired on enemy trenches - at the same time the 75th Battery fired on German guns in P.7 a.	R.P.

Army Form C. 2118.
23.

WAR DIARY
or
INTELLIGENCE SUMMARY.
(Erase heading not required.)

Instructions regarding War Diaries and Intelligence Summaries are contained in F.S. Regs., Part II. and the Staff Manual respectively. Title pages will be prepared in manuscript.

Hour, Date, Place	Summary of Events and Information	Remarks and references to Appendices
YPRES. March 10th.	The orders for the days programme were as follows:— Orders by Left Group Commander. 10.3.15 1. Our infantry in both sectors will open a heavy burst of rifle and machine gun fire at 12 noon today, lasting say 3 or 4 minutes. At 12.3 p.m. 18 pr batteries will open fire and take the following in objectives. <u>31st Bde</u> 2 Btles (a) German trenches in front of our trenches 36c.31. (b) A spot content of cutting T.35.b.27. where a machine is thought to be. 1 Battery "Short Range" T.35.C.17. 146 Bde. 1 Bty. German trenches to rear of Hill 30. 1 Bty. German trenches in front of our trenches 47.48. 1 Bty "Short Range" - P.y. a (N° 18) 3. At the above time H. salvos will be fired by each Bty. It is possible two rally may be directed by Red Fire to their rapid burst of fire and following bursts in addition to above. 11 a.m. - 1 p.m. 2 - 4 p.m. in which case the following will be sent you. "Cooperating in all bursts". 5. On receipt of this message you will make arrangements to be on send objectives at between 11 - 11.3 am 2 - 3 pm's 4 - 3 pm That time P. also ready from each battery on all time occasions. 6. Watches will be synchronised with H.Q.s of battalions to which F.A. Brigades are attached.	

WAR DIARY
or
INTELLIGENCE SUMMARY.
(Erase heading not required.)

Army Form C. 2118.

24.

Instructions regarding War Diaries and Intelligence Summaries are contained in F.S. Regs., Part II. and the Staff Manual respectively. Title pages will be prepared in manuscript.

Hour, Date, Place	Summary of Events and Information	Remarks and references to Appendices
YPRES. March 10th	1. If you are not called on to fire at 11.3 a.m. 6" salvos (limited of 4) will be fired at 12.3 pm from each battery.	
9.15 a.m.	Sgd. P.G. York, Capt. R.A. adjt. 8 Bde. RFA	
	2 Lieut. V.H. ⦵ Johnson joined the Brigade and was allocated to the 366 Battery	K.P.
March 11.	The three batteries fired salvos at intervals of one minute 11.3.15. Infantry batteries to them Received following Order:— Orders by Left Group Commander. 11.3.15.	K.P.
8.25 a.m. Empf 15 am	O.C. 14t Bde. 1. From 2.45 p.m. to 3 p.m. there will be continuous rifle and artillery fire, as fast as ammunition allows, along the whole front of the division. 2. The 18 pr. brigades of the group will fire on the German trenches in Kiel and artery zones. 3. Rate of fire as follows:— Each brigade will fire one salvo from each battery every two minutes commencing with	

Army Form C. 2118.
25

WAR DIARY
or
INTELLIGENCE SUMMARY.
(Erase heading not required.)

Instructions regarding War Diaries and Intelligence Summaries are contained in F.S. Regs., Part II. and the Staff Manual respectively. Title pages will be prepared in manuscript.

Hour, Date, Place	Summary of Events and Information	Remarks and references to Appendices
YPRES French 11ᵗʰ	3. 31ˢᵗ Bde at 2.46 146 " " 2.46 And finishing with 3. 31ˢᵗ Bde at 2.57 146 " " 2.58 Making seven salvoes to be fired in all from each battery of the group. 4. Duty line can be had from this office. 5. The 9ᵗʰ Bde relieved the 13ᵗʰ Inf. Brigade in this section last night. The 5ᵗʰ Fusiliers are holding the right section. The Liverpool Scottish are holding trenches 38, 39, 40 & 49. The 1ˢᵗ Scots Guards are holding 143 to 50 Bn 49. The last two battalions are in the same Bde as the 6. The O.C. Royal Fusiliers and Lincolns will be at Lt. Royfil Knoll. H.Q. Knoll Bde. Commander at tomorrow. Bde Cmdrs will kindly arrange to come also at above hour. 11. 40 a.m. P.G. Yorke Adjt. 8 Bde. R.F.A.	

Army Form C. 2118.

26

WAR DIARY
or
INTELLIGENCE SUMMARY.
(Erase heading not required.)

Instructions regarding War Diaries and Intelligence Summaries are contained in F.S. Regs., Part II and the Staff Manual respectively. Title pages will be prepared in manuscript.

Hour, Date, Place	Summary of Events and Information	Remarks and references to Appendices
YPRES March 11th 2.46 pm.	The batteries carried out the programme. At the end of the programme it was reported that the Germans were attacking Kink 40 and the batteries were ordered to fire on the German huts opposite Trench 40. This turned out to be a false alarm. Capt. C.A.R. Scott joined the Bde. and took over the command of the 366 Battery. 2nd. Lt. Greenfield joined from the 37th Battery R.F.A. and posted to 4 in 1 Col.	
March 12th 8.23 am to 9.13am.	The three batteries fired salvos at intervals of six minutes in accordance with programme for the day.	
2 pm to 2.30pm.	The 367 Battery and H.Q. Bde. were shelled by howitzer fire without suffering any damage. Late in the afternoon the German flare up & failure of the trenches in this sector and the batteries were ordered into trenches 44 to 47 in case of an attack but did not open fire as an attack was not made.	K.P.
March 13th	About 10 am. received "Short Range" message. "15" battery fired 3 salvos on pt. Squares I. 35. F.O.d. The three batteries opened on the enemy trenches and fired salvos at intervals of 4 minutes in accordance with the day programme.	Programme Sheet
2.22 pm.		

Army Form C. 2118.

27

WAR DIARY
or
INTELLIGENCE/SUMMARY.
(Erase heading not required.)

Instructions regarding War Diaries and Intelligence Summaries are contained in F.S. Regs., Part II. and the Staff Manual respectively. Title pages will be prepared in manuscript.

Hour, Date, Place	Summary of Events and Information	Remarks and references to Appendices
YPRES. March. 13. 2.34 p.m.	Batteries ceased firing	K.P.
March. 14th.	At intervals throughout the day from 9 am to 6.40 p.m. the batteries fired on enemy trenches and gun on receipt of "Short Range" messages from the infantry Bn. A.G.	
9.38. a.m.	The 367th & 75th Batteries fired salvos on enemy support trenches in front of ZWARTELEEN salient in accordance with programme received from Left Group Cmdr. —	K.P.
March. 15th 12.30 a.m.	Received message from Left Group Commander. "All Batteries must be on the alert at 12.45 as there will be a counter attack by 27th Divn at 1 o'clock." The night passed off quietly on this sector —	

Army Form C. 2118.

28

WAR DIARY
or
INTELLIGENCE SUMMARY.
(Erase heading not required.)

Instructions regarding War Diaries and Intelligence Summaries are contained in F.S. Regs., Part II. and the Staff Manual respectively. Title pages will be prepared in manuscript.

Hour, Date, Place	Summary of Events and Information	Remarks and references to Appendices
YPRES. March 15th 2.5 p.m.	The Battery fired on enemy's battery while the infantry had five minutes deliberate fire.	
2.10 p.m.	Fire ceased. Enemy returned our fire and shelled 367 Battery getting the range accurately. No casualties.	K.P.
March 16th 10.10 a.m.	Received tel. message from trench 46 to open fire.	
11.11½ a.m.	366 Battery fired with one round.	
10.12 a.m.	Tel. message from 49 trench to open fire.	
10.14½ a.m.	366 Battery opened fire. These messages came through Bn H.Q. when they could have gone straight back from the trench to the 366 Battery via the artillery wire.	K.P.
2.30 p.m.	367 and 98th Batteries fired 3 salvos each in rapid succession on Hill 60 & behind it.	K.P.

Army Form C. 2118.

29.

WAR DIARY
or
INTELLIGENCE SUMMARY.
(Erase heading not required.)

Instructions regarding War Diaries and Intelligence Summaries are contained in F.S. Regs., Part II. and the Staff Manual respectively. Title pages will be prepared in manuscript.

Hour, Date, Place	Summary of Events and Information	Remarks and references to Appendices
YPRES. March 17th 5½ p.m.	Received message from 39 Truck "Release 39 left."	
5.1 p.m.	369 Battery opened fire.	
4 p.m.	Received following message from Left Group hdqrs. To 146. Y369 17.3.18 Message from 38th Divn begins. G.319 17th. The following scale of gun ammunition will not be exceeded and if exceeded will not be made up from L. of C. AAA. 18br. three rounds per gun. 20 H.E. AAA. 4.5 Howitzer two rounds per gun no lyddite ends. In accordance with these instructions this scale will on no account be exceeded except in case of attack AAA No Searching fire guns with mobtened fire will be possible on the scale AAA Bde. Cmdrs. must judge if called on by infantry whether fire is necessary AAA. If they are in doubt they must refer matter to Left Group Commander before firing. 3.38 p.m. Col Duffus.	

WAR DIARY or INTELLIGENCE SUMMARY.

(Erase heading not required.)

Army Form C. 2118.

30

Hour, Date, Place	Summary of Events and Information	Remarks and references to Appendices
YPRES. March 18	No firing – 149 Battery brought on tractor into its new position tracter wheelday. (J.20.c.56.)	K.P.
March 19 11. a.m.	149 Battery commenced to register on Hill 60 –	The 149 Battery had originally been 22 A. battery.
11.30 a.m.	Proceeded registering on Hill 60.	
11.36.	Started to register on ZWARTELEEN.	
12.5 p.m.	149 Bty. completed range testing and returned to the wagon line of the enemy	
3.35 p.m.	36½ + 76 Battues used simultaneously on salvo each on the winter slopes of Hill 60. Snow closed all the morning.	K.P.
March. 19. 11. a.m.	149 Battery continued ranging on Hill 60. and ZWARTELEEN.	K.P.
12.5 p.m.	149 completed their ranging –	

Army Form C. 2118.

31.

WAR DIARY
or
INTELLIGENCE SUMMARY.
(Erase heading not required.)

Hour, Date, Place	Summary of Events and Information	Remarks and references to Appendices
YPRES. March 20. 1. p.m.	75th Battery shelled by Enemy's heavy battery. 10 rounds.	K.P.
2.45. p.m.	75th Shelled by enemy field guns. 6 rounds.	K.P.
March 21st 9 a.m.	Enemy aeroplane dropped a bomb which fell few yards from this house. No damage done. Following message received from H.Q. Group Commander:- "The G.O.C. R.A. wishes officers to realise what has become known to the General Staff. The weight of our attack at NEUVE CHAPELLE attracted German reserves to that locality from all along the line, notably two brigades from our immediate front. And had these Inf. Bdes. have now returned and are disposable for offensive purposes on our front of the enemy so also is Hence the necessity of ceaseless vigilance, dependable and quick communication, accurate and quick fire if called on. The Lt.Col Cundy the Group has told me to forward the above which was received verbally." Sgd. P.G. Yorke Capt adjt. 8 Bde R.H.A.	K.P.

21-3-15

WAR DIARY
or
INTELLIGENCE SUMMARY.
(Erase heading not required.)

Army Form C. 2118.

32.

Instructions regarding War Diaries and Intelligence Summaries are contained in F. S. Regs., Part II and the Staff Manual respectively. Title pages will be prepared in manuscript.

Hour, Date, Place	Summary of Events and Information	Remarks and references to Appendices
YPRES. March 22nd 6.15 p.m.	Received the news that PRZEMYSL had fallen — 15th Inf Brigade relieved the 9th Bde. on this sector.	K.P.
March 23rd 1.6 p.m.	367 Battery fired a salvo on 60 Hill where a Germany working party were seen.	
9.15 p.m.	Message from Left Group Commander to fire on German trenches opposite trenches 47 — 40. " " " " 47 " " " " 40 " " " " 45.	K.P.
9.14 p.m. 9.20 p.m.		
March 24th 12.37 p.m.	Message received from O.C. Bedfords to effect that enemy are shelling our 47 trench left left from this position. 367 K Battery fired two salvos on enemy battery in I.36.c.88.	K.P.

Army Form C. 2118.

33

WAR DIARY
or
INTELLIGENCE SUMMARY.
(Erase heading not required.)

Instructions regarding War Diaries and Intelligence Summaries are contained in F.S. Regs., Part II. and the Staff Manual respectively. Title pages will be prepared in manuscript.

Hour, Date, Place	Summary of Events and Information	Remarks and references to Appendices
YPRES. March 25.		
11.25 a.m. to 11.45 a.m.	387 Battery fired nine rounds on reverse slope of Hill 60.	
	During the afternoon the 78th Battery was heavily shelled by 8" shell. The enemy in it was very accurate. The only damage done was two rifles in a dug out shield and side of dug out blown in. All detachments had been withdrawn. In the evening the 78th Battery took up a new position further back. One section in T.15.b.4.6 and one section in T.15.a.7.9.	R.P.
March 26. 3.40 p.m.	Checkerboard message received from O.C. Cheshire Regt. that 50 Trench mortar battery shelled by mortar. 366 Battery fired at pt. I.30.c.10.7. and apparently silenced the mortar.	R.P.
	The 78th Battery registered one of its sections.	
March 27. 3.0 a.m.	387 Battery fired five salvoes Reg. Pt. I. 36.c.78 and stopped the shelling on our trenches. 2nd Lt. F.J. Cooper R.A. attached to K 149 Battery.	R.P.

Army Form C. 2118.

34

WAR DIARY
or
INTELLIGENCE SUMMARY.
(Erase heading not required.)

Instructions regarding War Diaries and Intelligence Summaries are contained in F.S. Regs., Part II and the Staff Manual respectively. Title pages will be prepared in manuscript.

Hour, Date, Place	Summary of Events and Information	Remarks and references to Appendices
YPRES. March 28. 11.7. a.m.	367 fired two salvos at I.36.c.78. 2nd Lieut. Glenwick posted to Bde and attached to 367th Battery.	K.P.
March 29. 9.30 a.m	Enemy shelled 367 Battery with high explosive.	K.P.
March 30.	367 Battery fired on enemy guns in redoubt in enemy line & kindus	K.P.
Noon to 12 n'n.	366 Battery fired on enemy guns near KLEIN ZILLEBEKE	P.P.
	B Battery fired on enemy redoubt.	
March 31.	Major T. Carlyon R.F.A. joined and was posted to 367th Battery vice Capt. B.V. Macdona	K.P.

121/5254

28th Division

146th Bde R.F.A.

Vol IV 1.4 — 30/4/15

Army Form C. 2118.

35

WAR DIARY
or
INTELLIGENCE SUMMARY.
(Erase heading not required.)

Instructions regarding War Diaries and Intelligence Summaries are contained in F.S. Regs., Part II. and the Staff Manual respectively. Title pages will be prepared in manuscript.

Hour, Date, Place	Summary of Events and Information	Remarks and references to Appendices
YPRES 1st April 1915	A quiet day.	R?
2nd		
11.6 a.m.	75th Battery (Left section) fired 2 rounds on KLEIN ZILLEBEKE battery.	
11.15 "	Right section of 75th Battery and 15th ECOLE shelled	R?
12.15 p.m.	was shelled by enemy. 75th Battery had one man wounded who died in hospital the same evening.	
3.30 p.m.	75th Battery right section again shelled - 8 shells in quick succession. This section changed its position in the evening.	R?
3rd		
2.49 p.m.	336 Battery fired Enemy guns been KLEIN ZILLEBEKE fired on enemy trenches on Hill 60.	R?
"	367 " "	
5th		
6.10 a.m.	367 Battery fired 3 salvos at German trench mortars by order of Left Group Cmdr. This mortar had caused considerable damage the previous day to trenches in the zone on our right.	R?
2.40 p.m.	367 fired on mortars.	

Army Form C. 2118.

36.

WAR DIARY
or
INTELLIGENCE SUMMARY.
(Erase heading not required.)

Hour, Date, Place	Summary of Events and Information	Remarks and references to Appendices
YPRES. April 7th		
3.32. p.m.	Following message received. "Relieve 8th Artillery 48."	
3.33	75th Battery fired on KLEIN ZILLEBEKE battery.	
6.38 p.m.	Following message received from Left Bn. H.Q. "S.O.S" The three batteries fired S.O.S on their own zones at once. The 366 Battery had previously opened fired upon hearing the sound of rifle fire from the left of our zone. The Brigade Commander then called up the left group commander in confirmation of S.O.S message & rifle fire having then ceased. "S.O.S N° 49 - 50." Then came back from the Left Group commander and the batteries opened fire on the targets 49 - 50.	K.P.
1.57 p.m.	The message "Steady, now normal." was received from Bn. H.Q.	
April 8th	Lieuts C.H. Marsh Roberts and J Jackson joined the Brigade on being posted to it.	K.P.

Army Form C. 2118.

37.

WAR DIARY
or
INTELLIGENCE SUMMARY.
(Erase heading not required.)

Instructions regarding War Diaries and Intelligence Summaries are contained in F.S. Regs., Part II. and the Staff Manual respectively. Title pages will be prepared in manuscript.

Hour, Date, Place	Summary of Events and Information	Remarks and references to Appendices
YPRES. April 8.	At night the advanced sections of the 15th Bde. R.F.A. 5th Div. Artillery came up to the commence taking over the position from the Brigade. One section of 52nd Battery relieved a section of the 78th Battery & one section of the 80th Battery relieved a section of the 366 Battery.	K.P.
April 9th 12.45 am 12.45 pm	The reliefs by the advanced sections & were completed. During the morning the Brigade less the section still in action and headquarters moved into temporary rest billets 1½ miles West of POPERINGHE. At night the remainder of the guns were relieved.	
April 10th 1.10 am	The whole relief by the 15th Bde - R.F.A. was completed. By 11 a.m. the whole of the 14th Bde. was back in billets.	K.P.
April 11th	The G.O.C. V Corps. inspected the Bde. on Church Parade and they made an address.	K.P.

Army Form C. 2118.
38.

WAR DIARY
or
INTELLIGENCE SUMMARY.
(Erase heading not required.)

Hour, Date, Place	Summary of Events and Information	Remarks and references to Appendices
April 11th	At night the 28th Divisional Artillery commenced to relieve the 39th French Divisional Artillery in the ZONNEBEKE sector of the line. The first half of the relief of this Bde. was completed before 12 midnight.	
April 12th	The second half of the relief was carried out at night and was completed.	K.P.
April 13th 12.19 a.m.	The whole relief by the 146 Bde. was completed and the batteries in their new positions. The 149 Battery came into action for the first time. This the 4th batteries of this brigade were now all in action. The Batteries registered during the morning. The 85th Infantry Brigade were in front of this Bde. The 2nd of this of the Bde. covered the 4th, left and centre Battalions being the Buffs.	K.P.
9.30 p.m.	The Batteries stood to the guns as an attack by the Buffs was expected arrived yesterday by the fire of the 367 Battery. The attack did not take place. The allowance of ammunition for the Bde. was now fixed at 332 rounds per week.	K.P.

WAR DIARY
INTELLIGENCE SUMMARY
(Erase heading not required.)

Army Form C. 2118.

39

Hour, Date, Place	Summary of Events and Information	Remarks and references to Appendices
ZONNEBEKE April 14. 9.0 p.m.	367th Battery fired 28 rounds in answer to an S.O.S. message from the Infantry in trench B2. A working party were repairing the trench when they were attacked by some Germans who got into the trench but were subsequently ejected.	N.P.
April 15th	Enemy mortar opposite B sector of our trenches very active.	
1 p.m.	367 Battery - & 149 Battery fired 32 rounds in conjunction with the 37th - 6.5" Howitzer battery standing down for enemy mortar - The 367th & 149th Batteries were the several occasions called upon to fire on German mortar during the day.	N.P. N.P.
April 16th	One section of the 69th Battery 31st Bde R.J.A. relieved one section of the 149th Battery after dark -	N.P.
" 17th	The remaining section of 69th Battery relieved the remaining section of 149th Battery.	N.P.

Army Form C. 2118.

40

WAR DIARY
or
INTELLIGENCE/SUMMARY.
(Erase heading not required.)

Hour, Date, Place	Summary of Events and Information	Remarks and references to Appendices
ZONNEBEKE. Ap. 17.	The first section of 149th Battery relieved a section of a French Battery of the 11th Division further North and W. of GRAVENSTAFEL.	
Ap. 18th 6.20 a.m.	The 84th Inf. Brigade asked for the assistance of the 367th Battery as they intended to make an attack north the Welsh Regt. on the Cross Road at BROODSEINDE which had been occupied by the Germans during the night. These cross roads were subjected to a heavy bombardment during the course of the morning & the Germans were shelled out - the infantry then worked into this trench but were in turn bombed out of it. — After dark the second section of 149th Battery relieved the remaining French section, and this Brigade formed the Left Artillery Group and came under the orders of the 85th Inf. Bde. — E.P.	

Army Form C. 2118.

41.

WAR DIARY
or
INTELLIGENCE SUMMARY.
(Erase heading not required.)

Hour, Date, Place	Summary of Events and Information	Remarks and references to Appendices
ZONNEBEKE. April 19. 5 p.m. 7 p.m.	The enemy made a resolute attack to regain Hill 60 taken from them by 15th Inf. Bde. 5th Div. on evening of 16th. The attack was supported by heavy gun fire accompanied by a bombardment of YPRES. The attack was unsuccessful.	K.P.
April 20.	Today orders were received to dump 200 rounds per gun retaliation. The 78th Battery which came out of action to rest on Sunday night was sent to the V Div. Artillery and came under the orders of G.O.C. R.A. V Div. Two guns came into action with 500 and 1800 yds of enemy trenches - in support of Hill 60.	K.P.
April 22. 7 p.m.	German attack north east of YPRES on right of French line and left of Canadians commenced. Enemy employed poisonous fumes and drove the Algerians only of their trenches. The Canadians left wing was thus compelled to swing back and the enemy broke through the gap. The 18th Battery thought the guns into action No th of WIELTJE and supported	K.P.

Army Form C. 2118.

42

WAR DIARY
or
INTELLIGENCE SUMMARY.
(Erase heading not required.)

Hour, Date, Place	Summary of Events and Information	Remarks and references to Appendices
ZONNEBEKE. April 21st	Three artillery officers from Kitchener Army attached to Brigade for 14 day's instruction - Lieut. Douglas Irvine attached 149 Bty. 2Lt. Dibdin 366 Bty - 2Lt Foulds 367 Batty. -	K.?
April 22nd 4 p.m.	The German attack preceded by the discharge of volumes of asphyxiating gas commenced - Position of Batteries of 146 Bde. as follows. 73rd Battery had two guns out to V Div'n on gun mules repair on gun with wagon line in WIELTJE. 149. 366. 36.7 Batteries were supporting 85th Inf Bde and facing East in square D8. D19.c. D20.b. respectively on the left of 85th Bde. were two Canadian Bdes which joined up with the French line in the neighbourhood of LANGEMARCK. The enemy broke through the night of the French line and the left of the Canadians was thus forced to throw back. This left a gap through which the enemy found through on St. JULIEN. The 149 Battery was left in a dangerous position with Germans close on its left rear - At this time there were Canadian 18 pr. batteries in D24.c. One battalion of 2nd Canadian Bde. which was in reserve was hurried up to fill the gap and assist the 3rd Canadian Bde. to make a counter attack	K.?

WAR DIARY
or
INTELLIGENCE/SUMMARY.
(Erase heading not required.)

Army Form C. 2118.

43.

Hour, Date, Place	Summary of Events and Information	Remarks and references to Appendices
ZONNEBEKE, April 22nd. 6.30 p.m.	on the line St. JULIEN and Wood in C.10.c. Major Fewer assisted by Lieut. Graham brought howitzer into action about 800 yds. N. of WIELTJE near the North Midland 4.7 heavy battery to support the Canadian counter attack. The Gun came into action under rifle fire. The men of the 4.7 Btty. had retired from their guns with the exception of one Officer and 2 N.C.Os who were removing the breech blocks. The counter attack commenced supported solely by the 75th gun which fired over a front of 20° to the N.	K.P.
11.30 p.m.		
April 23rd. 12.30 a.m.	The 149 Btty. was ordered to withdraw and come into Action N. of WIELTJE facing N. to support the Canadian 3rd Bde.	
3.30 a.m.	The Battery came into action 500x N of WIELTJE and was joined by the 75th gun which had come out of action at 3 a.m. having fired 280 rounds. During the day the 149 fired on various targets in support of the Canadians. The battery was under rifle fire at 1000 yds and heavy shell fire. The Canadian counter attack reached the N. edge of wood in C.10.c but eventually they were driven back.	K.P.

(73989) W4141—463. 400,000. 9/14. Fl.&J.Ltd. Forms/C. 2118/10.

WAR DIARY
or
INTELLIGENCE SUMMARY.
(Erase heading not required.)

Army Form C. 2118.

Hour, Date, Place	Summary of Events and Information	Remarks and references to Appendices
ZONNEBEKE. April 23.	During the day the remainder of the 75th Battery withdrew W. of canal and came under the direct orders of C.R.A. 28 Div. It came into action in I.1.a. and subsequently supported the French. The 366 and 367 Batteries were heavily shelled all day. On their recent throughout the day this Bde. was called upon by the Canadian Batteries to supply ammunition they having no knowledge of other then ammn. column was - Three Canadian batteries K.P. late in the day withdrew towards YPRES.	
April 24.	During the morning the 149 Battery position became untenable owing to heavy rifle fire and very accurate and heavy Howitzer fire. One gun and wagon being knocked out by direct hit.	
3. p.m.	The Canadian line fell back on the right front of the battery to within 700 yards and the enemy occupied ST. JULIEN. Communication was extended and the Battery Commander decided to withdraw the battery. This very difficult operation was completed by that night and the battery withdrew W. of the canal. One disabled gun and 5 wagons being left on the position it being impossible to get them away. In the evening the 149 came into action in I.1.a. near the 75th Battery.	

WAR DIARY
or
INTELLIGENCE SUMMARY.
(Erase heading not required.)

Army Form C. 2118.
45.

Hour, Date, Place	Summary of Events and Information	Remarks and references to Appendices
ZONNEBEKE April 24.	During the whole day the 366 and 367 Batts were heavily shelled.	
9. p.m.	In view of the situation at St JULIEN the O.C. 146 Bde R.A. received orders from C.R.A. 28 Div. to withdraw a section from each of the 366 and 367 Batteries and bring them into action facing N. near VERLORAN HOEK to support an attack by a fresh Inf. Bde. on St JULIEN at daylight on 25th. The 149 Battery was to support the left flank of the attack in the direction of the road in C.10.c. On the request solicitation of the R.E.s 366 & 367) and the O.C. 146 Bde brought the two sections in action facing N. in D.19.b. This action was approved of by the C.R.A. 28th Div.	R.P.
25.K	The 10th Inf Bde crumbs attacked on St JULIEN and eventually established itself on the line from FORTUIN westwards across ST JULIEN road at C.17.d.3.4. The 11th Inf. Bde. was ordered up on the night of the 10th and to be in position by 9 pm connecting up with the left of the 85th Bde in N.10.d in D.10.c.	
7.30 p.m. 4 Z.W.	The Bde received orders from C.R.A. to get in touch with 10 & 11th Bde. Arties and support their attack. The 366 & 367 again heavily shelled. One section of 367 had a whole detachment killed wounded except one man.	R.P.

WAR DIARY
or
INTELLIGENCE SUMMARY.
(Erase heading not required.)

Army Form C. 2118.

46.

Hour, Date, Place	Summary of Events and Information	Remarks and references to Appendices
ZONNEBEKE April 26. 4 a.m.	During 6 the situation about the GRAVENSTAFEL ridge the positions of the 366 and 387 Batteries became very serious. The Canadians were falling back and the 11th Bde. had left the front the left of 8's Bde. A second gap in the line appeared through which the enemy were advancing on ZONNEBEKE. The 366 Battery was engaging enemy infantry at 800 yds range. The section of 387 Btty. in Square D.20.b. which is a position in C.30.c.	
6 a.m.	The guns of the 387 facing North were withdrawn to a position in C.29.c. The remaining guns being withdrawn about midday. During the day strong reinforcements arrived and in the afternoon the 11th Inf. Bde. established the trench line down FORTUIN to wood in D.10.c. assisted by reduced battalions of 28th Div.	
8.30 p.m.	The 4 Guns of (36) Btty moved forward & occupied positions as follows. One section in Square D.20.a. facing N. and one sect in D20.c. facing E. - P.S. The 366 & 36) Batteries fired incessantly from daylight onwards under very heavy shell fire all the time from two directions.	
27th.	The 145? Btty. was asked to report its Bde. in support of 85 Bde. It came into action in I.5.d. but was at-	

WAR DIARY
or
INTELLIGENCE SUMMARY.
(Erase heading not required.)

Army Form C. 2118.

47.

Instructions regarding War Diaries and Intelligence Summaries are contained in F.S. Regs., Part II. and the Staff Manual respectively. Title pages will be prepared in manuscript.

Hour, Date, Place	Summary of Events and Information	Remarks and references to Appendices
ZONNEBEKE. April 27th	Been shelled from the rear. In the evening this battery came into action in D.19 near 37th How. battery. The position proved to be untenable and the battery shot their guns. Under instructions from C.R.A. the sections of 65th How. Btty. was transferred from left group to right group night group to left group and came under the orders of OC 146 Bde. — Capt. C.F. Ward found and posted to 75th Battery.	
28th 2.30 a.m.	The two sections of 366 & 367 faery E. with sect. of Hows. supported a counter-attack by a portion of 85th Bde (parties of Sherwoods, K.O.Y.L.I., E. Surreys & 8th Middlesex) in which 25 in the clerk of which the enemy had established Hindeland on the Monday. The 149 Battery withdrew in daylight. During his withdrawal the battery had to cross about 3/4 mile of ground in full view of the enemy. It was done at a gallop under shell fire but only the casualty — The battery came into action in C.29.e. covering a front of 2000 yds. to the N.E. Lieut. Stewart 366 Battery was wounded during the morning at the Observing Station and one gun of 366 was knocked out by direct hit.	

Army Form C. 2118.

WAR DIARY
or
INTELLIGENCE SUMMARY.
(Erase heading not required.)

Instructions regarding War Diaries and Intelligence Summaries are contained in F. S. Regs., Part II. and the Staff Manual respectively. Title pages will be prepared in manuscript.

Place	Date	Hour	Summary of Events and Information	Remarks and references to Appendices
ZONNEBEKE	April 28th		Throughout the day the sections facing North and How. Section fired a various objectives in support of 11th & 85th Bde.	R.P.
	April 29th		Nothing of importance occurred. Lieut. Foulds attached to 367. wounded in head.	
	30th		Soon after daylight Lieut. Hay-Neff - 366 Bty. was wounded while putting out a fire in one of the dug outs. The gun teams of 367th Battery were shelled in a farm in C.30.B. The farm caught fire and 4 gun limbers and 15 horses were destroyed.	

Mr Cordery.

P.A. with 146th
Bde. R.F.A. diary.

Eastmem

Original returned
17/4/25.

WINCHESTER 615.

PRIORS BARTON,
WINCHESTER.

16 April 1925

Dear Sir.

In case it maybe of any use to you I enclose a copy of a rough diary of 12 days during the 2nd battle of Ypres. It is perhaps a little interesting as the 149th Battery RFA was only formed a few weeks before from two sections of other batteries and was disbanded later when 6 gun batteries were reformed in Macedonia.

The battery formed a unit of 146th Bde, and at the time mentioned in the diary was commanded by myself as a Captain.

I have not touched up the diary since it was written & it is rather crude, but it gives a rough idea of the confused fighting after the German gas attack.

Yours truly
R.S. Ellis
Major

CXLVI Bde. R.F.A.
28th Division.

TELEGRAMS:
KNIGHTON, PLYMOUTH.
STATION: PLYMSTOCK,
SOUTHERN RY.

AGENT:
COLONEL G. R. T. RUNDLE, C.B.

LANGDON ESTATE OFFICE,
KNIGHTON,
PLYMSTOCK,
S. DEVON.

21st Nov 1925

Dear Edmunds.

I have had a search for my Ypres Diary but owing to so many moves since 1915 I have mislaid it, but I have my map with the various positions of my batteries marked at the time of the actual gas attack 22nd April and afterwards during the fight.

On 22nd April 1915 —

149 Battery (Ellis) D. 14 b 6,9, 600 yards from the Cross Roads at Gravenstafel

75 Battery (Jervis) in Camp near St JEAN. & WIELTJE
N.G.M
had only 2 guns available, remainder under repair.

366 Battery (Capt. E.W. Ffrench / Wickham) D 20 a 8,4
T.E.

367 (Carlyon.) D 20 c 7.9.
/T

Ellis withdrew his battery after dark and came back to Wieltje & went into action just north of that village, as you have his diary you will know his subsequent movements. You can rely on what he wrote at the time

Any of these Battery Commanders might be able to give you information, or my adjutant at that time, Capt. S. D Graham, now a Captain & at the Staff College.

As you will know from the Official records our G.O.C. Bulfin & Gay (CRA 28 Division) were all back at Poperinghe when the actual gas attack took place, & I never got any orders from Gay throughout the battle & was left to my own initiative as to targets etc.

I had one of the Canadian batteries under my temporary command in D 19 a 2.2. 2 other Canadian batteries were in C 24 b 8.5. All these 3 batteries ran out of ammunition and withdrew behind Ypres on the 23rd or late on the 22nd anyway my batteries were the only ones on the left of the line on the original front as on the 22" April at 5 PM.

The 75 Battery was shelled out of its billet retired across the Canal & was loaned to another division

& I saw nothing of it until we
went out of the line on the 29 April.
The 37th Battery (Howitzers) under Harding
Newman (now CRA of a division in India)
brought his battery up I think on the
24th. Came into action somewhere
N. of FRIEZENBERG, & I sent Ellis'
Battery there also, but, as all the gun
positions in that neighbourhood were
visible to the Germans, Harding Newman
implored me to withdraw the 149 in Battery,
for fear of giving his position away;
his objection was St Julien almost
entirely. The French had cleared
all this area of trees & hedges whilst
they reoccupied this line up to April 1915,
so that it was very difficult to find
any gun positions that were in
any way screened. The 149 Battery as Ellis's diary
may relate, had to continually shift its position it was pushed
into from the rear at one position it took up.
Most certainly gave all the
    orders to fire on St Julien. (There
    was no one else to give any)

I was in touch with the infantry
& acted on the information they
gave me.

I cannot remember the hour
when I ordered all the (3) batteries
to fire at St Julien, but it was
our chief objective, so I think I/we
can safely say that we did fire
on St Julien in the forenoon of the
24th

Carlyon & Wickham would help you
I am sure, they had a very strenuous
time.

I am wrong in saying Wickham
was in command of the 366th Battery,
he had been wounded just previously
(E.W.T. ffrench)
& his Captain (Temporary) took his place,
until he was wounded on the 25th "99"
I hope these rough notes may be of use.
Most of the incidents of those days are
still after a lapse of 10½ years vividly
engraved on my memory.
Should I find my diary & if not too late
I will certainly forward it to you —
I should like to read the German official
account of the 1st Gas attack.
Yours sincerely, L.A.T. Rundle

COPY.

FROM COLONEL G.R.T. RUNDLE, C.B., (CXLVI Bde R.F.A. 28th Division.)

Re 2nd YPRES.

Langdon Estate Office,
Knighton,
Plymstock,
S. Devon.

21st November, 1925.

Dear Edmonds,

I have had a search for my Ypres Diary but owing to so many moves since 1915 I have mislaid it, but I have my map with the various positions of my batteries marked, at the time of the actual gas attack 22nd April and afterwards during the fight.

On 22nd April 1915:

149 Battery (Ellis) D.14.b.6.9. 600 yards from the Cross Roads at Gravenstafel.

75 Battery (Jervis N.G.M.) in camp near St. Jean and Wieltje had only 2 guns available, remainder under repair.

366 Battery (Wickham T.E.) [Capt. E.W. French] D.20.a.8.4.

367 Battery (Carlyon T.)   D.20.c.7.9.

Ellis withdrew his battery after dark and came back to Wieltje and went into action just north of that village; as you have his diary you will know his subsequent movements and you can rely on what he wrote at the time.

Any of these ~~three~~ Battery Commanders might be able to give you information, or my adjutant at the time, Capt. S.D. Graham, now a captain and at the Staff College.

As you will know from the official records our G.O.C. Bulfin and Gay (C.R.A. 28th Division) were all back at Poperinghe when the actual gas attack took place, and I never got any orders from Gay throughout the battle and was left to my own initiative as to targets etc.

I had one of the Canadian batteries under my temporary command in D.19.a.2.2. Two other Canadian batteries were in C.24.b.8.5. All these three batteries ran out of ammunition and withdrew behind Ypres on the 23rd or late on the 22nd. Anyway my batteries were the only ones left on the left of the line on the original front as on the 22nd April at 5 p.m.

The 75th Battery was shelled out of its billet and retired across the Canal and was loaned to another division and I saw nothing of it until we all went out of the line on the 29th April.

The 37th Battery (Howitzers) under Harding Newman (now C.R.A. of a division in India) brought his battery up I think on the 24th and came into action somewhere N. of Frezenberg and I sent Ellis' battery there also, but, as all the gun positions in that neighbourhood were visible to the Germans, Harding Newman implored me to withdraw the 149th Battery for fear of giving his position away; his objective was St. Julien almost entirely. The French had cleared all this area of trees and hedges whilst they occupied this line up to April 1915, so that it was very difficult to find any gun positions that were in any way screened. The 149th Battery, as Ellis's diary may relate, had to continually shift its position, it was fired into from the rear on one position it took up.

I most certainly gave all the orders to fire on St. Julien (there was no one else to give any).

I was in touch with the infantry and acted on the information they gave me.

I cannot remember the hour when I ordered all the (3) batteries to fire at St. Julien, but it was our chief objective, so I think you can safely say that we did fire on St. Julien in the forenoon of the 24th.

Carlyon and Wickham would help you I am sure, they had a very strenuous time.

I am wrong in saying Wickham was in command of the 366th Battery, he had been wounded just previously and his captain (temporary - E.W. Ffrench) took his place, until he was wounded, on the 25th ??

I hope these rough notes may be of use. Most of the incidents of those days are still, after a lapse of 10½ years, vividly engraved on my memory.

Should I find my diary and if not too late I will certainly forward it to you.

I should like to read the German official account of that gas attack.

Yours sincerely,

G.R.T. RUNDLE.

Notes in ink by Major Becke.

COPY.

> Priors Barton,
> WINCHESTER.
> 16th April 1925.

Dear Sir,

In case it may be of any use to you I enclose a copy of a rough diary of 12 days during the 2nd Battle of Ypres. It is perhaps a little interesting as the 149th Battery R.F.A., was only formed a few weeks before from two sections of other batteries and was disbanded later when 6 gun batteries were re-formed in Macedonia.

The battery formed a unit of 146th Bde., and at the time mentioned in the diary was commanded by myself as a captain.

I have not touched up the diary since it was written and it is rather crude, but it gives a rough idea of the confused fighting after the German gas attack.

> Yours truly,
> (sd) R.S. ELLIS,
> Major.

149th BATTERY R. F. A.

22. 4. 15. Battery in position just North of HONEBECK brook in D.8. facing East Target, German trenches on the railway to Wood 40, in support of the Royal Fusiliers.

During the late afternoon German attack on the North reached as far as the village of ST. JULIEN in rear of the Battery position. I sent back to our wagon lines five miles in rear for the teams to come up in readiness. At midnight I got orders from O.C. 146th Brigade to withdraw my battery to a position North of WIELTJE and get into communication with Canadian Headquarters in C.22 to support our line facing North. The Battery came into position in C.22.D about 3.30 a.m. and General Turner, Commanding 3rd Canadian Brigade asked me to fire on the North end of the big wood in C.10 and any visible targets.

23. 4. 15. During the day I fired on various roads and houses to the North, observing my fire. The left of the Battery and the Observation Station were under direct rifle/fire and machine-gun at a range of about a thousand yards. I had no visible targets as it was very uncertain which trenches were held by us or the Germans.

24. 4. 15. Canadian Headquarters could give me no information, simply telling me that the Germans were moving into ST. JULIEN and asked me to fire on visible targets. During the morning the rifle fire became worse and I fired on houses at ranges of 1400 and 1900 yards. During this time the Battery had been ranged upon a Battery of German Howitzers which eventually got the exact range and line, one gun and wagon being hit. Having no more targets I moved the detachments to a flank and waited for further targets. At about 3 p.m. Canadian Headquarters informed me that their line was falling back to a position on my right front about 700 yards from the Battery, which line they hoped to hold till dark. About this time I had a message from O.C. 146th Brigade to fire on ST. JULIEN and act as I thought best.

I turned two guns on ST. JULIEN and fired by the map until all ammunition was exhausted. As it was impossible to bring up more ammunition and the position of the Battery was precarious, I decided to try and withdraw the guns. As the first two teams came up the position was heavily shelled, several horses were killed and one complete team was killed while getting away. I waited half an hour and got two more guns away without casualty. This left one intact gun and one completely disabled gun and three wagons (one broken) on the position.

I had had five guns in action as one gun of the 75th Battery had joined me on the 23rd.

Having no more teams available near the position I collected all my detachments and went back to the wagon line to collect the Battery together, teams and vehicles being very much scattered and disorganized by shell fire.

One team, under 2/Lt. Game went back to the position to attempt to get out the last gun. I moved the Battery meanwhile to another position and came into action just West of the Canal in I.1.A. facing North-east about 7 p.m.

The team which had been to fetch the gun joined me there with the report that 2/Lt Game had been wounded and they were unable to get the gun.

As soon as it was dark another team with some gunners under 2/Lt. Russell went back to get the gun, which they succeeded in doing without coming under fire. I reported my movement to the C.R.A. and also that I had left one completely disabled gun, three wagons and two gun limbers empty on the position, and was told by him not to attempt to withdraw these wagons. I was also ordered to place myself in communication with O.C. 75th Battery who was away in action on my left. I myself then rode to 146th Brigade Headquarters and reported my action during the day and the present position of the Battery.

The casualties officially notified during the day were, two

drivers killed and one officer and thirteen N.C.O's and men wounded.

25.4.15. I registered on German trenches and houses and farms in C.14.D. and C.9.B. and was given a zone in conjunction with the 75th Battery, 365th Battery, and two Belgian batteries in support of French troops.

26.4.15. The Ammunition Column had completed me with horses and three ammunition wagons. I had four guns in action (one of the 75th's). Between 1 p.m. and 2 p.m. I fired on German front line trenches and supports in my zone in support of a French attack which advanced at 2.5 p.m. This advance in my zone was met by volumes of asphyxiating gas and did not succeed, the troops falling back to their own trenches without a rifle shot being fired.

During the early morning of this day we had orders to fire on German supports after the failure of an earlier attack by the French.

27.4.15. After a quiet night I was sent for to R.A. Headquarters where I received orders from C.R.A. to move Battery at once to near VERLDRENHOEK and get in touch with my own Brigade with a view to helping the 85th Infantry Brigade. I came into action in D.15.D with an Observation Post in D.29.B. and the Battery was fired upon from the rear (South) before we fired a shot, one man being wounded. Under orders from O.C. Brigade I then went forward to reconnoitre a position in D.19 near 367th and 366th and 37th batteries who were facing East, North, and West and occupying the only area of ground not directly visible to the enemy.

I chose what seemed a covered position not knowing the ground very well, with a view of firing on my old zone between the railway and Wood 40. During the night I brought the Battery, (3 guns) into action. O.C. 37th Howitzer Battery immediately telephoned away saying that if I fired a shot it would render the whole area untenable and I was ordered not to fire except in emergency.

28.4.15. I had orders from O.C. 146th Brigade to withdraw the Battery at once in daylight, which I did. During this withdrawal the Battery had to cross about three quarters of a mile of ground in full view of the enemy. It was done at a gallop under shell fire with only one casualty. I brought the Battery into action close to the Brigade Headquarters in C.29.C. with an Observation post in a dug-out in C.29.B., registered on German front line trenches to the North-East, covering a front of 2,000 yards in front of the 11th Infantry Brigade.

NOTE. In all these latter positions I only took the guns into action, with no wagons or limbers.

29.4.15.)
30.4.15.) Desultory firing on my zone and enemy's gun positions located
1.5.15.) by aircraft. During this time the wagon lines and the approaches to the position were under continual shell fire.
(During this time I received a new gun and the gun of the 75th Battery left me to rejoin).

2.5.15. Germans were everywhere reported massing in my zone and to the East and West of it, and we fired a lot during the day and night of the 2nd/3rd.

3.5.15. In the early morning the Battery was shelled from its right flank by "Whizz-Bangs" and ranged upon by heavy howitzers. Later in the morning I had orders to shell the line of the ZANEBECK BROOK where the enemy were reported to be collecting for the attack. Very soon after opening fire the Battery was shelled by 8-inch Howitzers with exact range and one gun was disabled. Several times we got into dug-outs and waited for the shell-fire to cease, but every time we fired again they opened on us, and I decided to try and find another position. We hauled the guns out by hand, limbered up behind the farm and got two guns into a new position. As we were laying out the lines we were fired upon from the South by Howitzers, the shells falling within two yards of the guns. This was about 5 p.m.

I then received orders for the withdrawal in the evening, and as there was no position which was not observed by the enemy, either from North, East, or South, I collected the Battery together by degrees into the wagon line near YPRES. We left the wagon line at 9.30 p.m. and marched to POPERINGHE with three intact guns, one disabled gun, six ammunition wagons, one G.S. wagon, and one broken water cart.

During these twelve days, we reported two drivers killed, one subaltern and nineteen N.C.O's and men wounded, of which were two Sergeants, one Corporal, two Bombardiers. We had twenty-five horses killed and twenty-three wounded, two guns disabled by gun-fire, one of which was abandoned, and five wagons smashed or abandoned.

(sd) R.S. ELLIS.
Captain, R.F.A.
Commanding 149th R.F.A.

5.5.15.

121/5481

28th Division

146th Brigade R.F.A.

Vol II / II — 30.5.15

A.
AG

WAR DIARY or INTELLIGENCE SUMMARY

Army Form C. 2118.

Place	Date	Hour	Summary of Events and Information	Remarks and references to Appendices
	May 1st		Lieut. Lynch joined and posted to 366 Battery.	
	" 2nd	5 p.m.	The Enemy attacked the 10th Inf. Bde on the line ST. JULIEN - Bois de Cuisiniers. Heavy volumes of poisonous gas preceded the attack. All 3 batteries fired in support and the attack was unsuccessful. During the morning on instruction from C.R.A. two sections of the 3rd Bde. R.G.A. (under Col. Walker) were placed round N. to help the 146 Bde.	
		3.30 p.m.	Orders received to withdraw at night the section the battery to an area near POPERINGHE. Owing to the gravity of the situation these order were cancelled and the battery remained in their positions	

WAR DIARY
or
INTELLIGENCE SUMMARY.

Army Form C. 2118.

49.

Hour, Date, Place	Summary of Events and Information	Remarks and references to Appendices
ZONNEBEKE. May 2nd.	On this day the "A" left section of 369 Battery was rendered practically useless owing to overwhelming shell fire from two directions. They turned their same remark applies to the 366 battery. Enemy massing to attack all along the line. All through the day the 146 Bde. was incessantly called upon to detach with its fire 10", 11" and 83" Bdes. This involved covering a front of 8000 yds. and fire was incessantly kept up chiefly by map on various targets in enemy's lines. The guns were under a terrific hostile shell fire all the time and observation of fire was rendered almost impossible owing to telephone wires continually being cut and struck from enemy shells. Lieut. Lynch, 366 Battery was blown to pieces while at the Observing Station. The following Tull- Dalton and Connor, 367 Battery were wounded and the 149 Battery had one gun knocked out.	
4.30 p.m.	Orders received from C.R.A. 28 Div." to withdraw the Bde. at 9.30 p.m. to rest area west of POPERINGHE.	
9.30 p.m.	The Bde. withdrew without any casualties and went into rest area early next morning.	

Army Form C. 2118.

50.

WAR DIARY
or
INTELLIGENCE SUMMARY.
(Erase heading not required.)

Instructions regarding War Diaries and Intelligence Summaries are contained in F. S. Regs., Part II. and the Staff Manual respectively. Title pages will be prepared in manuscript.

Hour, Date, Place	Summary of Events and Information	Remarks and references to Appendices

During the 12 days fighting from 22nd April to 3rd May the Bde. was on the lett and was called upon to fire on a front of 8000 yds.
The Bde. fired during this period 12000 rounds.
The casualties to the Bde. were as follows:-
Officers. 1 killed. 7 wounded.
N.C.Os & men. 7 killed and 70 wounded.
Horses. 111 killed and wounded
4 guns disabled by shell hits.
5 wagons abandoned and disabled.
4 gun limbers burnt.

The 365 and 367 Batteries of the German advance of 22nd April were shortened to 6500 yards of our own trenches just in front and upon hostile shell fire the whole time. Rifle bullets also from enemy's line came into the batteries.

H.P.

Army Form C. 2118.

57

WAR DIARY
or
INTELLIGENCE/SUMMARY.
(Erase heading not required.)

Instructions regarding War Diaries and Intelligence Summaries are contained in F. S. Regs., Part II. and the Staff Manual respectively. Title pages will be prepared in manuscript.

Hour, Date, Place	Summary of Events and Information	Remarks and references to Appendices
POPERINGHE May 4th	Arrived in rest-billets in square L.23. S.W. of Poperinghe. The gun arrived from base 366 Battery. 30 horses and 14 mules arrived for Brigade.	K.P.
" 5th	366 Battery sent one gun to 31st Bde.	K.P.
" 7th	The Bde. sent 4 guns to 31st and 3rd Brigades. and	
" 8th	12 amm. wagons from the column.	
" 10th	One gun arrived from base for 149 Battery.	
" 13th	A draft of 28 mules arrived for the Bde.	K.P.
" 9th	2nd Lieut. L. Wood and 2nd Lieut. Herbert joined the Bde. and posted to 366 & 367 Batteries respectively.	
" 13	Draft of 35 mules arrived for Bde. Draft of 22 gunners & 12 drivers.	K.P.
" 15th	Capt. C.F. Ward killed in action on duty in in the trenches as observing officer.	K.P.
" 16th	2/Lt. F.C. Corbin & F.E. Wood joined Bde.	K.P.
" 19th	Capt. Ellis taken in hospital with fever (malarial).	K.P.
" 20th	2nd Lt. R.P. Waller attached to Bde. from Kitchener army for fortnight instruction	K.P.

Army Form C. 2118.

52

WAR DIARY
or
INTELLIGENCE/SUMMARY.
(Erase heading not required.)

Hour, Date, Place		Summary of Events and Information	Remarks and references to Appendices
POPERINGHE	May 22nd	Capt. K. Parbury took over command of 149 Battery R.F.A. during absence of Capt. Ellis and Lt. S.D. Graham took over duties of Adjutant.	R.I.P.
	23	No test.	
YPRES	24	Moved up to north of canal in support of 85 Infantry & took up position in advance of any other guns.	SATR
"	25	In front of delivery the 149, & 366 Batteries were dug in & 30 am 367 Battery having lent two guns to the Batteries was ammunitioned. Lt. F.V. Bowater (Sp: Res.) & 2nd Lt. Brown (Imp.y Com 3) joined for duty. 1 wounded & 366 & 112 other ranks at 2.C.	SATR
	26	Reg. ordering. The other section moved up during the night & the 25-26 SATR.	
	27th	Zones of batteries altered making registration necessary again. Quiet day.	STG
	28th	Quiet day. 85th Inf. Bde. relieved by 9th Inf. Bde. in the evening. 149 & 366 Bty positions in sg-	STG
		I. 3.c	
	29th	Quiet day. STG	
	30th	Quiet day. 9.30 pm one section of 24th Bty	STG
		RFA relieved one section of 149 Bty.	
		10 pm. 1 Section of 34th Bty relieved one section of 366 Bty	STG

121/5871

28th Division

146th Bde R.F.A.

Vol VI   31.5. — 30.6.15

Army Form C. 2118.

53

WAR DIARY
or
INTELLIGENCE SUMMARY.
(Erase heading not required.)

Hour, Date, Place	Summary of Events and Information	Remarks and references to Appendices
N. WINNEZEELE May 31st	Quiet day. In evening remaining section of 149 & 366 Btys. relieved by sections of 2nd & 734th Btys. 75th Btys. remaining section relieved by 72nd Bty. and returned to Bde. - Bde. marched to rest area 3 miles W. of WATOU. during night of 31st - 1st. Hunt Walker left the Bde. - In rest. - Light cases of typhoid in the Amm. Col. believed to be due to a carrier.	S.T.G.
June 1st, 2nd		S.T.G.
3rd	12-noon. Parade dismounted under Major T. Carlyon in honour of H.M. the King for whom three cheers were given. Col. Rundle to Hospital sick.	
4th 11.30 a.m.	Maj. Gen. Bulfin G.O.C 28th Divn. addressed the Bde. (less Amm Col.) on the work they did in the YPRES Salient.	S.T.G.

WAR DIARY
INTELLIGENCE SUMMARY.
(Erase heading not required.)

Army Form C. 2118.

54.

Hour, Date, Place	Summary of Events and Information	Remarks and references to Appendices
June 7th	Major N.G.M Jenn returned from leave and assumed command of the Bde.	P.S.G.
" 14th	Col. Pundall returned and assumed command of the Bde in forenoon.	S.S.G.
" 17th	4.50pm. One Section from each battery and A.C. marched to DICKEBUSCH and relieved corresponding section of 47th Bde R.F.A. Capt J. FALLEN posted to command Am. Col. from Div A.C. All section of batteries registered trenches —	S.S.G.
DICKEBUSCH June 18th	HQs took over from HQs. 47th Bde at noon. In evening remaining sections relieved corresponding sections of 47th Bde. Also Am Col — Billets taken over, especially A.C. & HQ, found very unsanitary —	P.S.G
June 19th	Remaining section registered. Bde attached for duty to V.th Division & placed under O.C 30th Bde R.F.A. Lt.Col. STAVELEY (Group Commander)	P.S.G

Army Form C. 2118.

55

WAR DIARY
or
INTELLIGENCE SUMMARY.
(Erase heading not required.)

Instructions regarding War Diaries and Intelligence Summaries are contained in F.S. Regs., Part II. and the Staff Manual respectively. Title pages will be prepared in manuscript.

Hour, Date, Place	Summary of Events and Information	Remarks and references to Appendices
DICKEBUSCH June 19th	Battery. Position. Wagon Line.	
	146 Bde Hqrs. H29c19 H28d95	
	76th N4a45 H31d59	
	149th N.4a55 H31a32	
	366th H.34b25 H31d45	
	367th I26b32 H31d37	
	A.C. H25d5.0	
June 20th	Quiet day. Btys fired 32 rds. at Trenches.	18F.
21st	Quiet day. Btys fired 32 rds. " "	18F.
	2/Lt. A.C. STRACHAN joined Bde and posted to 75th Bty	
22nd	Quiet day. Bde fired 15 rds.	18F
23rd	" " " " 51 rds.	S.F.
	Midnight O.C. 5th Bde R.F.A. Lt.Col. DUFFUS relieved 30th Bde R.F.A. and assumed command of Right Group. 5th Division.	S.8.F.
24th	2/Lieut. C.H. MARSH-ROBERTS and Lieut. F.A. COOPER transferred to French Howitzer Battery and struck off strength of the Bde accordingly.	S.8.F.

Army Form C. 2118.

56

WAR DIARY
or
INTELLIGENCE SUMMARY.
(Erase heading not required.)

Instructions regarding War Diaries and Intelligence Summaries are contained in F.S. Regs., Part II. and the Staff Manual respectively. Title pages will be prepared in manuscript.

Hour, Date, Place	Summary of Events and Information	Remarks and references to Appendices
JUNE 24th	Quiet day. Btys fired 15 rds. Mentioned in despatches dated May 31st 1915. Col. G.R.T. RUNDLE. Capt. C.W. HINCE (Ac) Capt. R.S. ELLIS (14984) No. 29416 Co/Sjt G.A. DAZZELL (H.Qs.)	S.X.F.
25th	Btys fired. 25 rds. — Col. RUNDLE made C.B. in list of Birthday honours — 366 Bty fired at trench mortar	S.X.F.
26th	All batteries registered on points in their area to supply enemy. 51 rds fired	S.X.F.
10am to 12.30pm 27th	12.45 am to 1.30 am 366 fired 7 rds at Trench Mortar. Batteries registered on points in neighbourhood of the Mound. 85 rds fired	S.X.F.
28th	75s 366 & 367 Btys fired 6 rounds each in neighbourhood of the Mound according to Programme received from D.C. R.A. Corps. 77 rds fired	S.X.F.
29th	Programme of Registration repeated. 34 rds fired. On Trench much annoyed by Whiz 33 bangs – 367th Battery retaliated.	S.X.F.

Army Form C. 2118.

57

WAR DIARY
or
INTELLIGENCE SUMMARY.
(Erase heading not required.)

Hour, Date, Place	Summary of Events and Information	Remarks and references to Appendices
1915 JUNE 30ᵗʰ	Registration continued by order of O.C. Right Group. 59 rds fired during 24 hours. German whiz 33 bangs active R & T Sector. 369 Bty retaliated.	S.S.9.

28th Division.

146th Bde R.F.A.

Vol VIII

Army Form C. 2118.

WAR DIARY
or
INTELLIGENCE SUMMARY.
(Erase heading not required.)

58.

Instructions regarding War Diaries and Intelligence Summaries are contained in F.S. Regs., Part II. and the Staff Manual respectively. Title pages will be prepared in manuscript.

Hour, Date, Place	Summary of Events and Information	Remarks and references to Appendices
1915 JULY 1st.	Programme of Registration continued. Fog interfered somewhat. 59 rds fired.	P.S.G.
2nd	Registration 10am. 6.p.m. 30am. 31 rds fired.	P.S.G.
3rd	Registration 10am. 6.p.m. 30am. 49 rds "	S.I.G. / P.S.G.
4th	Registration 10am & 11.30am. 24 " "	
5th	German fired on KRUISTRAAT HOECK return points in the neighbourhood — no fixed registration for Batteries to-day. 31 rds fired.	S.S.G.
10pm	149 put one gun in prepared emplacement in German trenches at range 9'300.*	
	O.1.a.3.7. 16 fire on German trenches. 19 rds fired.	
6th	Quiet day.	P.S.G.
7th	Fairly quiet day. 149 Bty's forward gun fired 6 rds. at 4 p.m. 2 direct hits 4/pm. Enemy's whizz bangs active. Bty fired 50 rds.	S.S.G.
8th	Enemy's whizz bangs active in morning. 149 Bty forward gun fired 17 rds. midday. Bty. fired 45 rds.	P.S.G.

WAR DIARY
or
INTELLIGENCE SUMMARY.
(Erase heading not required.)

Army Form C. 2118.
59

Instructions regarding War Diaries and Intelligence Summaries are contained in F.S. Regs., Part II and the Staff Manual respectively. Title pages will be prepared in manuscript.

Hour, Date, Place	Summary of Events and Information	Remarks and references to Appendices
JULY. 9th	Quiet day - Bcn fired 33 rds.	P.S.G.
10th 3.30 a.m.	4 mines (ours) exploded opposite Q, & R, Trenches. 75th, 366th & 367th Batteries fired in communication trenches in vicinity. Intermittent fire kept up by 367th on German working parties in & by 367th on German exploded opposite R. Crater formed by mine exploded opposite R. Rifle mine was very successful & blew away about 75 yds of German trench. Up to 12 noon 576 rds fired 149 1364 formed gun fired 24 rds at German parapet getting 10 direct hits. 11.30 - 12.15 pm 3 pm Bombardment of DICKEBUSCH by Germans. 4.30 am Bombardment of Q, R, & Seely Trenches by 9th in 33 Lamps & heavy guns - KOYLI called upon 367th to fire as Germans were appearing to get ready for an attack. 61 rds fired by 367, other batteries fired a few rds too. Bcn fired 10 3 rds up to 12 noon.	P.S.G. P.S.G.
11th		

WAR DIARY
or
INTELLIGENCE SUMMARY.
(Erase heading not required.)

Army Form C. 2118.

60

Hour, Date, Place	Summary of Events and Information	Remarks and references to Appendices
JULY.		
12th	Quiet day. Batteries fired 10 rds w/p K 12 noon	PJS
13th	" " " 36 "	PJS
14th	" " " 49 " "	
	Forward gun of 149 Bty fired 30 rds &	
	did a good deal of damage to German	
	parapet. One man wounded 366 Bty	
	kept line by German naval gun mounted 1.S.S.	
15th	Quiet day. 4 " Rds fired up to 12 noon	PJS
16th	" " 27 " " "	
	9.30 pm one section from each battery & 1 Section	
	A.C. withdrawn and took up new positions.	
	25th from 1 Battery 3rd Northumbrian Bde	
	other batteries from 1st " "	
	Sections from 27th Bde RFA replaced these	
	Sections.	
17th	27th Bde RFA took over command at	PJS
	DICKE BUSCH at 12 noon.	

Army Form C. 2118.

WAR DIARY
or
INTELLIGENCE SUMMARY.
(Erase heading not required.)

Hour, Date, Place	Summary of Events and Information	Remarks and references to Appendices
DRANOUTRE.		
July 17th 1915.	9.30 pm Remaining Section of Bde withdrawn & took up new position.	S.T.G.
	6 pm. C.O. assumed command in new position.	
18th	Change completed & all batteries in position at 1.40 a.m. Registration of sections during the day. Lieut. COOLEY wounded in head in D.4 Trench.	S.T.G.
19th	Registration. Quiet day. 361st fired from 28. Div. Gr. Tk. 149. Bde AE. 56 rds.	P.S.P.
	Lieut. D.S. FOSTER	P.S.P
20th	" Quiet day. 30 "	
21st	" " 30 " "	
22nd	COL. RUNDLE left the Bde. MAJOR P. de BERRY assumed command of the Bde. 6 pm. Lieut. P.M. HOSACK joined Bde reported to 75th Bty. Lieut A.S. MEYRICK WAITES " " 366 " Lieut H.G. YEARSLEY attached to 149 "	S.T.G.
23rd	Quiet day.	
24th	Quiet day.	S.T.G

WAR DIARY
or
INTELLIGENCE SUMMARY.
(Erase heading not required.)

Army Form C. 2118.

62

Hour, Date, Place	Summary of Events and Information	Remarks and references to Appendices
JULY 25th	Quiet day. 77 rds fired.	C.S.F.
26th	Quiet day. Enemy working party in KEMMEL batteries. Hits observed on the Spinach batteries.	S.S.F.
27th	Batt HQrs shelled N33d1.5 12 noon. Quiet day. Usual registration and German working parties in neighbourhood of WYTSCHAETE fired at. 40 rds fired. One man wounded in 366 Bty. 5 rds fired.	S.S.F.
28th	Quiet day. 67 rds fired.	S.S.F.
29th	Quiet day. 3rd Bde (temporarily attached) registered German trenches with enfilade fire. 62nd Bty fired Trenches opposite C, D, & E Trenches as far as	S.S.F.
30th	SPANBROKMOLEN. During afternoon 3.30 a.m. Heavy gun fire heard from direction of HOOGE. 36 Rds fired. Lieut H. V. HOSACK (Special Reserve) joined Bde and posted to HQrs accdnly of his C.S.F.	

(73989) W4141-463. 400,000. 9/14. H.&J. Ltd. Forms/C. 2118/10.

121/6737

35th Division

146th Inf Bde R.F.A.
Vol VIII
August 15.

WAR DIARY
INTELLIGENCE SUMMARY
(Erase heading not required.)

Army Form C. 2118.

63

Hour, Date, Place	Summary of Events and Information	Remarks and references to Appendices
July 31st	A shoot was carried out by the 75's & 366's Batteries, observation being taken from a balloon. Hostile German artillery rather more active than usual.	S.S.G. / S.S.G.
August 1st	A quiet day. Brigade fired 41 rounds.	S.S.G.
August 2nd	A quiet day. Brigade fired 26 rounds.	S.S.G.
August 3rd	A moderately quiet day. " " 30 " fired.	
4th	" " 38 " "	
5th	Quiet day. In the evening one section of 149 Bty relieved one section of 162nd Bty in their enfilage position 78 c 44	S.S.G.
6th	Quiet day. 149 Bty completed their move by 10 p.m. 65 rds fired	S.S.G.
7th	Orders received to save ammunition - 35 rds fired	
	Quiet day. A/49 Bty joined the Bde (4. 4.5" How's)	S.S.G.

Army Form C. 2118.

64

WAR DIARY
or
INTELLIGENCE SUMMARY.
(Erase heading not required.)

Hour, Date, Place	Summary of Events and Information	Remarks and references to Appendices
Aug. 8th	3 & 3.40 am demonstration by Divisional Artillery against SPANBROEK MOLEN. 366134½ fired 570 rds. 149 By fired 48 rds. A/49. 366134½ 367 fired 259 rds. Poor show – very misty all the time	P. S. G
9th	Quiet day	
	6 to 7 pm days trench mortar bombing D trenches from about N. 36 a 9.5 . 366 7149	E S G
	By fired, then A/49 By. mortar caught in 9 pm red rocket sent up by Carham	S S G
10th	Quiet day.	S S G
11th	G.O.C. 28th Division inspected A/49. 75th, 366 and 367 Batteries commencing 10 am	
12th	Nothing doing. Bde hardly fired a shell LT. M.M. CRUICKSHANK R.A.M.C. relieved LT. A. D. VERNON-TAYLOR as M O of the Bde.	S S G
13th	Quiet day –	P S G

Army Form C. 2118.

65

WAR DIARY
or
INTELLIGENCE SUMMARY.
(Erase heading not required.)

Hour, Date, Place	Summary of Events and Information	Remarks and references to Appendices
Aug 14th	Quiet day. A/149 Bty fired 20 rds. Shots at loophole opposite trench 14. At request of infantry who thought it was for a found projector.	PSP
15th	3 to 4 pm. Divisional tests of A/149 — 149 & 366 Batteries. Results fairly satisfactory.	PSP
16th	Quiet day. Guns were run to 75°, 366, 367 Amplitest. 1 gun of A/149 Bty did an experimental shoot against concrete emplacement. Results good.	PSP
17th	Quiet day. Genl Munster visited the Div. Genl Kitchener & Baruck had munsta visited the Divisionl & officer & 30 O.R. detailed for parade. 11 am. Was LoCRE. Batteries tested from C.O's. O.P. by CRA. Results good 2 to 3 pm	PSP
18th		PSP

WAR DIARY or INTELLIGENCE SUMMARY.

Army Form C. 2118.
66

(Erase heading not required.)

Hour, Date, Place	Summary of Events and Information	Remarks and references to Appendices
August. 19th	Machine gun emplacement fired on by reqmnt of infantry N.36.d.15. A/49 Bty got one direct hit.	S.T.G.
20th	Quiet day. A/49 reported two targets with balloon observation.	S.T.G.
21st	During afternoon German shelled C & D trenches with what 3.3 hows. 75th Bty retaliated.	S.T.G.
22nd	Retaliation by 75th Bty during afternoon for enemy's whizz bangs on C trench.	S.T.G.
23rd	366 Bty demolished German machine gun emplacement at N.36.d.28 getting 12 direct hits out of 24 rds fired.—4 p.m.	S.T.G.
24th	Quiet day. Enemy shelled behind D trench, S.T.G. during the morning with 6.9" guns.	S.T.G. / S.T.G.
25th	Quiet day.	S.T.G.
26th	" "	S.T.G.
27th	" "	S.T.G.

Army Form C. 2118.

6/

WAR DIARY
or
INTELLIGENCE SUMMARY.
(Erase heading not required.)

Instructions regarding War Diaries and Intelligence Summaries are contained in F. S. Regs., Part II. and the Staff Manual respectively. Title pages will be prepared in manuscript.

Hour, Date, Place	Summary of Events and Information	Remarks and references to Appendices
August 28th	Quiet day.	S.S.G.
29th	Quiet day.	S.S.G.
30th	Quiet day.	S.S.G.
31st	Quiet day.	S.S.G.

121/7018

28th Division

146th Bde R.F.A.

Vol IX

Sept. 15.

Army Form C. 2118.

65

WAR DIARY
or
INTELLIGENCE SUMMARY.
(Erase heading not required.)

Hour, Date, Place	Summary of Events and Information	Remarks and references to Appendices
Sept. 1st	Quiet day. In evening Germans reported digging a trench in front of their pie trench in V.1.a probably to enfilade Cun9. an trencher.	S.S.P.
2nd	Above trench registered by 75.5 Bty.	S.S.P.
3rd	Rain all day. No firing.	S.S.P.
4th to 12th	Quiet.	
13th	Large movement in German lines opposite D3 fired on by 149 Bty in morning & afternoon. 20 shrapnel & 4 HE expended. A/130 How Bty also fired 8 S. & 12 lyddite shrt. Lieut. P.S.C. CAMPBELL - JOHNSTON. A/130 Bty wounded while observing by a rifle grenade. 2nd Lt SAUNDERS of 366 Bty who was telephone operator being killed.	S.S.P.
17th	Continued shoot with 9.2" How. at Engine behind SPANBROEK MOLEN. 366 & 149 Bty followed up each of these rounds with salvos at communication and reserve trenches in neighbourhood.	S.S.P.

Army Form C. 2118.

69

WAR DIARY
or
INTELLIGENCE SUMMARY.
(Erase heading not required.)

Hour, Date, Place		Summary of Events and Information	Remarks and references to Appendices
Sept.	18th	Lights distributed by trench mortar & Rifle Grenades during night.	
	19th	366 7149. Fired at intervals. 13th, 14th, 15th, 16th C.F.A. Batteries arrived & took over 1 section each from 149. 75. 366 & 367 respectively. Relief completed.	SS
	20th	5.50 p.m. Canadian Section registered.	SS
	21st	Relief of Batteries & column completed by Canadian 4th Bde C.F.A.	SS
	22nd 10 a.m.	Bde marched to rest billets just N of MERRIS and told the ready to march at one hours notice.	SS
	26th 7.30 p.m.	Gen. Bde marched to billets at ESSARS arriving the orders to billet at MERVILLE having been changed en route to BETHUNE	PS

Army Form C. 2118.

WAR DIARY
or
INTELLIGENCE SUMMARY.
(Erase heading not required.)

Instructions regarding War Diaries and Intelligence Summaries are contained in F. S. Regs., Part II. and the Staff Manual respectively. Title pages will be prepared in manuscript.

Hour, Date, Place	Summary of Events and Information	Remarks and references to Appendices
BETHUNE 29th	B.C's & C.O proceeded to CAMBRIN to 57th Bde. R.S.A. to learn ground with view & taking over.	P.S.O
SEPT. 30th	One section of each battery relieved 1 section of each of 57th Bde. Batteries. Guns use 146 Bde. ammunition. Command exchange of changed.	P.S.O
OCT. 1st	Bty's fired on German trenches round KF.30 pm. completed. LITTLE WILLIE hined while our infantry assaulted. At second assault 1st WELCH Regt. took the whole trench and the end that connect the trenches at HOHENZOLLERN.	P.S.O P.S.O

(73989) W 4141—463. 400,000. 9/14. H.&J.Ltd. Forms/C. 2118/10.

121/7429

28th Division

146th Bde RFA
Vol X
Oct 15

WAR DIARY
or
INTELLIGENCE SUMMARY.

(Erase heading not required.)

Army Form C. 2118.

Hour, Date, Place	Summary of Events and Information	Remarks and references to Appendices
CAMBRIN. Oct 2nd	A good deal of bombing and infantry fighting in LITTLE WILLIE Trench all the morning. 75/15 & 149 & 367. Kept up barrage of fire on DUMP Trench & FOSSE Trench & the DUMP under orders from G.O.C. 54 Inf Bde. 3 p.m. About 50 of our men seen retiring from LITTLE WILLIE across the open into our old front line Trench. 8 p.m. & 8.30 p.m. above three batteries fired on MAD POINT, FOSSE Trench, and MADAGASCAR. Repeated from 9.45 to 10.10 p.m. for infantry assault at 9 p.m, which did not come off. Repeated from 9.45 to 10.10 p.m assault did not take place till midnight & without any artillery support.	S.X.F.
Oct 3rd	Batteries kept up a steady fire all day on FOSSE Trench, LITTLE WILLIE, Mad Point, North & South Face. Our infantry relieved out of HOHENZOLLERN Redoubt during the day. German crumpled on front line heavily during afternoon. 10.30 p.m. 75 & 8.30 p.m. 149 kept up 40 rds an hour on North	
Oct 4th	Face and Trench 367 on Northern Half of little willie between North Face, Little willie & little willie Attack at 6 & 5 a.m failed owing to inadequate artillery support.	P.S.

WAR DIARY
or
INTELLIGENCE SUMMARY.
(Erase heading not required.)

Army Form C. 2118.

72

Hour, Date, Place	Summary of Events and Information	Remarks and references to Appendices
CAMBRIN. Oct. 4th.		
	11 am 2 Batteries opened fire in LITTLE WILLIE and area just East of it. 35 rds per hour per battery. Rn 75. 149. 367 Batteries took turns 6 hours on 15 off.	P.S.
3rd	Lieut E. MAY joined Bde & posted K.A.C.	
	Fire continued all day & night. rate of fire being reduced at 12 noon to 15 rds per btry per hour.	P.S.
5th	Germans Stinson relieved an infantry in the trenches. Fire continued on German trenches, one battery on/per 6 hours at a time 30 rds per hour.	S.S.
6th & 8th	fire on trenches continued.	
	5.30 pm Germans reported attacking BIG WILLIE all batteries opened rapid fire on N. FACE. FOSS 8 Trench Attack repulsed by Grenadier Guards.	S.S.
9th & 11th	light was quiet.	
	Usual bombardment of German trenches. targets registered by aeroplane observer.	S.S.
13th	10 am 12 noon bombardment on HOHENZOLLERN Redoubt commenced mines attached - gas set off at 1 pm. assault at 2 pm Infantry entered Redoubt without firing a shot They retreated from it but returned	P.S.

WAR DIARY
or
INTELLIGENCE SUMMARY.

(Erase heading not required.)

Army Form C. 2118.

73.

Hour, Date, Place	Summary of Events and Information	Remarks and references to Appendices
14ᵗʰ	15 mins later. 2ⁿᵈ phase continued till 3.5pm. And the last phase till 12.30am. Very enquiry about the success of the attack which never got beyond the HOHENZOLLERN REDOUBT now held. Our batteries then came back on to FOSSE Trench & LITTLE WILLIE & CORONS ALLEY.	
	7pm 1 gun of 75 Bty had muzzle blown off by a premature HE which burst in bore. No casualties.	B.G. / P.G.
15ᵗʰ 87001 76.F. 17ᵗʰ	G⁺ FULLER 366 Bty killed in QUARRY. Slow rate of fire kept up on FOSSE Trench.	P.G.
	5am. Enemy attacked DUMP Trench & BIG WILLIE with bombs. Batteries fired on FOSSE Trench.	P.G.
18ᵗʰ/19ᵗʰ	Fairly quiet. Batteries fired on enemy working parties. Orders received to relieve burnt down, but later cancelled.	P.G.
19ᵗʰ	First section of 76 Bde R.F.A. relieved our section J 14.9. 366 & 367 Btys.	P.G.

Army Form C. 2118.

74

WAR DIARY
or
INTELLIGENCE SUMMARY.
(Erase heading not required.)

Hour, Date, Place	Summary of Events and Information	Remarks and references to Appendices
CAMBRIN. Oct. 20th	Relief of batteries completed by 76 Bde. R.F.A. 75th B.G. was not relieved by us & then Bde. marched to billets at ÉCLEME	PS/-
21st	All batteries and HQ entrained at VILLERS for MARSEILLES. A.C. on 23rd	PS/-
24th	Battery arrived at MARSEILLES and encamped in PARC BORELY. Camp very	PS/-
26th	Crowded and congested. A.C. arrived in Camp.	PS/-
Till 31st	Bde. remained in Camp.	

"A" Form.
MESSAGES AND SIGNALS.
Army Form C. 2121.

| Prefix | Code | m. | Words | Charge | This message is on a/c of: | | Recd. at | m. |
| Office of Origin and Service Instructions | | | Sent At ___ m. To By | | Service. (Signature of "Franking Officer.") | | Date From By | |

TO { 3 Bde / ~~110~~ / HB }

Sender's Number	Day of Month	In reply to Number		A A A
* BM 477	30th			

The relief of first section
of batteries will take place
tonight & will be complete
by 6.0 PM aaa HQ of
each Battery & one complete
section will reach BEVRY at
4.0 PM aaa BEVRY is in
F14c Sheet 36 B aaa Your
Co. will be informed &
orders will meet you ~~treat~~ at
BEVRY aaa acknowledge

From RonRa
Place
Time 2.0 PM

The above may be forwarded as now corrected.   (Z) [signature] for RFA
                                                 Censor. Signature of Addressee or person authorised to telegraph in his name.

* This line should be erased if not required.

OC 3rd Bde
Bde ? B de
146th Bde

SECRET

BM478

30.9.15

(1) Provided the situation permits - the responsibility for covering the front of the 28th Division will be assumed by the CRA of that Division + by his Brigade & Battery Commanders at 12 noon, tomorrow the 1st October.

(2) Brigade & Battery Commanders will be prepared to assume this responsibility + orders will be issued tomorrow stating whether the situation is favourable or unfavourable for their taking over.

(3) The batteries will consist partly of 9th Divnl + partly of 28th Divnl Artillery.

(4) Remainder of Batteries should move up early tomorrow morning - under Brigade arrangements - to their new areas.

(5) BACs will assume responsibility for the supply of Ammn at 8.0 AM tomorrow + must be moved up in the early morning to their new areas.

(6) acknowledge

M Fergusson May BMRA
4.40 PM

1. Copy No 3

28th Divisional Artillery
Operation Order No 47

Reference Sheets 36 B &c.   28.9.15.

(1). When the situation permits the 28th Divisional Artillery will relieve the 9th Divnl Artillery as under:-
  50th Bde will be withdrawn.
  The 146th Bde will relieve the 51st Bde
  The 3rd Bde (less 18th Bty) will relieve the 52nd Bde
  The 130th How Bde will relieve the 53rd How Bde.

(2) Bde Commanders, adjutants, battery commanders & one officer per battery will report tomorrow 8AM at the HQ of the Bde which they will relieve.
  HQ 51st Bde is at Chemists Shop CAMBRIN A19d7.2½ [36c]
  HQ 52nd Bde is at ANNEQUIN F29d7.0 [36B]
  HQ 53rd Bde is at ANNEQUIN at S.E. corner of Workmen's Cottages F29d6.3 [36B]

(3). Battery officers will go to the battery which they will relieve & learn everything to enable them to take over.
  All officers will make themselves acquainted with the situation.

(4). Attachment will take place from day to

2.

day. It is left to the discretion of Bde Cmdrs whether officers remain with the 9th Divn battalions at night, provided arrangements can be made which are acceptable to the Bde in question.

(5) Bde Cmdrs will make a verbal report to the CRA at 6.0 P.M. at RAHQ BETHUNE — unless they wish to remain out at night, in which case a written report will reach RAHQ at 6.0 P.M.

(6) Acknowledge.

6.0 P.M.

M. Fergusson.
Maj BM.RA.

Copy No 1 filed
    2 3rd Bde
    3 74th Bde
    4 130 (How) Bde

Progress Report. 149 Battery R.F.A.

6 am to 6 pm 2-10-15.

No fresh work on the enemy's defences has been observed.

Parties of the enemy were seen crossing the open from Lone Farm to PEKIN Cottages, & back again to LONE Farm - at intervals during the day.

At 2.55 pm the enemy started bombing LITTLE WILLIE Trench and at 3.5 pm our infantry vacated the trench.

The enemy's bombers seemed to have worked up some communication trench.

At 3.15 the enemy were seen in LITTLE WILLIE Trench. At 4 pm this bombing party got only LITTLE WILLIE Trench and made toward HOHENZOLLERN, & continued bombing.

At 4.30 pm further observation was impossible owing to fog.

R Parbury.
O.C. 149 Bty
R.F.A.

To O.C 146 Bde

BM 507. 4.10.15

The Corps direct that the trenches & areas under mentioned be kept under intermittent Artillery fire day & night.

Parapets should be destroyed especially on WEST FACE.

Objectives are allotted as under

3rd Bde 3 Batteries WEST, NORTH & SOUTH Faces & area between last two named.

Fire should not be brought beyond G.4.b.40 on WEST FACE.

2 Batteries 36 Bde FOSSE & DUMP Trenches as far SOUTH as point 60.

Also ground in triangle FOSSE Trench Little Willie NORTH Face.

2 Btys. 146 Bde

LITTLE WILLIE and triangle LITTLE WILLIE, NORTH Face FOSSE Trench. Shells should be dropped within 100ˣ of NEW Trench, which our men hold.

Occasional rounds from 130 Bde will be put into FOSSE COTTAGES, CORON MARON & PEKIN.

18 pdr Batteries will fire at rate of 30 rounds per hour.
Shooting will commence on receipt of this order.
H. E. will be used.
Acknowledge.

                B.M. RA.
                1.25 pm.

Copy No 4

28th DIVL ARTY   O.O   No 50

3rd Oct. 1915

1. The 83rd Infantry Bde will assault WEST FACE from point 60 to junction of Communicating Trench at G 4 b 1.2 at 4.30 a.m. tomorrow.

2. Artillery fire will be maintained all night as follows.

146 Bde   one Battery Northern half of LITTLE WILLIE; but 100 yards North and South from the junction of NEW TRENCH will be avoided.

one Battery North FACE TRENCH and to search open ground, included in triangle FOSSE TRENCH – LITTLE WILLIE — NORTH FACE.

3rd BRIGADE   One Battery SOUTH half of LITTLE WILLIE and WEST FACE down to G 4 b 1.2

One Battery WEST FACE to G 4 b 3.0, and not EAST of that point.

One Battery DUMP TRENCH between points 42 and 60 and to search open ground between North and South face, but not to shoot within 250 yards of point 60.

C BATTERY/130th BDE to fire 10 rounds an hour (spread out) into HOHENZOLLERN Redoubt, searching about.

3. Rate of fire for 18pr Batteries 40 rounds an hour, but rate at no time to be faster than one round a minute.

4 Acknowledge

8.50p.m.   C.R. Burkhardt Capt
                    f/ Bde Major R.A.
                           28th Division

Copy No 1   28th DIVISION
Copy No 2   1st CORPS
Copy No 3   3rd BDE R.F.A
Copy No 4   146th Bde R.F.A
Copy No 5   R.A (file)

13th
146 Bde
36th

Secret

BM495

2-10-15

(1) LITTLE WILLIE, having fallen into German hands during the day, will be retaken by assault by the 84th Infantry Brigade at 9.0 PM precisely.

(2) The Divisional Artillery will cooperate as under:
3rd Brigade DUMP TRENCH as far South as G5a26. South end of FOSSE COTTAGES & NORTH FACE between G4b9.7 & G4b6.5.
146th Brigade MAD POINT, MADAGASCAR and FOSSE TRENCH.
36th Brigade PEKIN ALLEY & FOSSE TRENCH.

(3) Fire will be opened at rate of Battery fire one minute at 8.0 PM. 9.45.
10.10 At 8.10 PM the rate will be increased to battery fire 20 seconds.
10.30 At 8.30 PM the fire will cease.

(4) Acknowledge by wire

6.17 PM.

W. Fergusson
Maj BMRA

OC 3rd Bde
136 Bde
146 "
5/6 "

SECRET
B.M.428?2
1.10.15
1-10-15

(1). At 8.0 P.M. precisely - the 84th Infty Bde will assault LITTLE WILLIE.

(2). A programme for heavy artillery support has been arranged.

(3). The Divisional Artillery will open fire at 8.0 P.M. as under:-
One battery 146th Bde on MAD POINT + MADAGASCAR.
Two batteries 146th " on FOSSE TRENCH.
3rd Brigade on DUMP TRENCH as far South as G5a2.6.
50th Brigade on PEKIN ALLEY

(4). Batteries will maintain a rate of fire of Battery fire 30 Seconds until 8.30 P.M.

(5). Acknowledge.

3.10 P.M.

M.Fergusson.
Maj BmRA
28.

"It must be understood that the preparation for the assault is to be carried out by the Heavy Artillery. The Divnl Artillery opens fire - on points in rear, at the moment the assault is delivered.

"C" Form (Original). Army Form C. 2123.
MESSAGES AND SIGNALS. No. of Message..........

Prefix... Code... Words...	Received	Sent, or sent out	Office Stamp.
£ s. d.	From......	At............m.	
Charges to collect	By........	To......	
Service Instructions. L Williams 11-0 P.m		By 1-9-15	

Handed in at................................Office............m. Received............m.

TO	O C 146 Bde R Sct

*Sender's Number	Day of Month	In reply to Number	
	1-9-15		A A A

We	have	the	whole	of	LITTLE
WILLIE	& the	bit	that		connects
the	trenches	at	HOHENZOLLERN		

FROM: F O O 146 Bde

PLACE & TIME:

* This line should be erased if not required.

28th Divisional Artillery   Copy No. 8

Operation Order No. 41.

19.9.15

1. The reliefs of the 2nd sections of the batteries to be relieved will be carried out as under :-

   146th Brigade on night 21st/22nd

   3rd and 31st Brigades on night 22nd/23rd

   under arrangements to be made between brigade Commanders.

2. The batteries of the 3rd and 31st F.A. brigades which are not relieved - and the 130th Howitzer brigade - will be withdrawn on the night 22nd/23rd.

3. The first sections of the 146th brigade, relieved tonight, will move tomorrow - the 20th instant - at 4.0 p.m., under brigade arrangements to H.26.c.1.1., where they will remain until their back area is definitely allotted. The Headquarters and second sections, when relieved on night 21st/22nd will proceed to the same position and move on the following day to their back area.

4. The first sections of the 3rd and 31st brigades - relieved tonight will move at 4.0 p.m. on the 22nd instant, under brigade arrangements to their back areas. The second sections of these batteries will, when relieved on night 22nd/23rd proceed direct to their back areas.

5. The batteries of the 3rd and 31st brigades which will not be relieved and the 130th Howitzer brigade will be withdrawn on the night 22nd/23rd to their wagon lines and will proceed to their back area the following day.

6. Half the 18-pounder sections of the 31st and 146th brigade A.C. will be relieved by half the 18-pounder sections of the 80th and 4th C.F.A. Brigade A.C's on the afternoon of the 20th and 21st respectively, the relieved sections remaining in their present lines.

2.

7. The S.A.A. Sections and remaining half of 18-pdr. Sections of the 31st and 146th Brigade A.C's will be relieved by the S.A.A. Sections and the remaining half of the 18-pdr. Sections of the 80th and 4th C.F.A. Brigade A.C8s on the morning of the 21st and 22nd respectively. The relieved Sections will remain in their present lines.

8. The four Brigade Ammunition Columns will move on 23rd to the back area.

9. The back areas will be allotted by the Staff Captains of the Infantry Brigades to which the Field Artillery Brigades are affiliated.

The D.A.C. and the 130th Howitzer Brigade come under the 84th Infantry Brigade for the purpose of billeting. Brigade and L.A.C. Commanders must get in touch with the Staff Captains of the affiliated Infantry Brigades without delay.

10. Acknowledge.

10.40 pm.m

Major
Brigade Major, R.A. 28th Divn.

Copy No. 1 filed.
Copy No. 2 28th Division.
Copy No. 3 17th Division.
Copy No. 4 2nd Canadian Division.
Copy No. 5 4th Canadian Division.
Copy No. 6 3rd Brigade R.F.A.
Copy No. 7 31st Brigade, R.F.A.
Copy No. 8 146th Brigade, R.F.A.
Copy No. 9 130th Brigade, R.F.A.
Copy No. 10 Divl. Ammn. Column.

Table showing Positions to be taken over by 28th Divisional Artillery.

Divisional Front   Canal to A 3 c 2.9

31st Brigade will take over from 9th Brigade.

Zone - Canal to A 9 centre.

103rd Battery	from	66th Battery	A 13 b 5.4
160th Battery	..	28th Battery	F 11 d 3.3
69th Battery	..	20th Battery	F 18 a 4.9
118th Battery	..	- Battery	F 10 d 9.4
Headquarters			F 10 b 0.4

146th Brigade will take over from 13th Brigade.   Headquarters BREWERY CORNER.

Zone A 9 centre to A 3 c 2.9

149th Battery	from	19th Battery	F 4 b 2.0
367th Battery	..	2nd Battery	F 5 b 4.3
75th Battery	..	7th Battery	F 11 b 2.6
366th Battery	..	B/87th Battery	X 24 c 6.3

130th Brigade.   Headquarters - LE QUESNOY CHATEAU

Whole Front.

C/130th Battery	from	61st Battery	F 5 c 3.5
A/130th Battery	..	- Battery	F 5 c 3.9
3rd Brigade Headquarters - LE QUESNOY FARM	)		
1 Battery 130th Brigade	)	Rest area.	

Second Phase.   2.0 p.m. to 2.10 p.m.

3rd Brigade.

   1 battery - DUMP TRENCH

   1 battery - Raise fire off WEST FACE on to A 28 d 9.0 to G 4 b 9.7

   1 battery - Raise fire off NORTH FACE on to FOSSE COTTAGES

   1 battery - Raise fire off SOUTH FACE on to DUMP TRENCH 97 to 35

146th Brigade.

   1 battery - Lift off Northern Half of LITTLE WILLIE on to Trench
                 from A 28 d 4½.7 - 9.0 Then from 2.10 p.m. to 2.30 pm
                 on Trench A 28 d 1.5 - A 28 d 4.8

   1 battery - CORONS ALLEY

   1 battery - FOSSE TRENCH

36th Brigade.

   As for first phase

22nd Brigade.

   As for first phase

Howitzers. 130th Brigade.

   1 battery - MAD POINT   ) From 1.45 p.m. to 2.30 p.m. 200 rounds of
) Lachrymatory shell then continue with
   1 battery - MADAGASCAR   ) lyddite till 4.0 p.m.

   1 battery - AUCHY LA BASSEE at 1.0 p.m. at slow rate till 1.45 p.m.
                 At 1.45 p.m. on front row of FOSSE COTTAGES with 100
                 rounds Lachrymatory shell till 2.0 p.m. then back on
                 AUCHY LA BASSEE with lyddite till 5.30 p.m.

64th Brigade.

   As for first phase except one battery (lift off HOHENZOLLERN REDOUBT
   on to FOSSE TRENCH 15 to 97)

Third Phase.   From 2.10 p.m. to 4.10 p.m. after 4.10 p.m. continued
                at section fire 1 minute, till 5.30 p.m.

146th Brigade.

  3 batteries - A 28 c 4.8 to A 22 d 8.4 (1 battery from 2.30)

36th Brigade.

  1 battery - A 28 b 1o.7 to A 28 b 7.4

  2 batteries - A 29 b 4.2 to A 30 a 7.4

22nd Brigade.

  3 batteries - on PEKIN Trench A 30 a 8.8 - A 30 a 7.4 - A 30 a 7.1. -
                  A 30 c 10.6

3rd Brigade.

  3 batteries - Barrage A 29 b 7.1 across open to A 30 c 7.2

  1 battery - A 29 a 7.2 to A 29 b 4.2

Howitzers. 130th Brigade.

  The batteries on MAD POINT and MADAGASCAR will at 4.0 p.m. fire on trench
  A 28 c 4.8 to railway at A 28 a 9.8

64th Brigade.

  1 battery - A 28 b 7.4 through LONE FARM along trench to A 29 a 5.6

  1 battery - A 29 b 2.4 to A 29 b 4.8

  1 battery - A 29 a 5.6 to A 29 b 2.4

Secret.

Amendment to Tables of Rates and Distribution of Fire.
----

1. The Infantry will now be withdrawn from BIG WILLIE to a point G 5 a 2.0 prior to the bombardment.

2. The 3rd Brigade Battery which fires on WEST FACE will extend its zone to cover the whole of WEST FACE to POINT 60 where it joins BIG WILLIE.

3. The battery 64th Brigade will in addition to bombarding points 32 and 33 bombard also trench running from points 32 to point 1.1 and 33 - 2.4 in WEST FACE.

4. At commencement of bombardment from noon to 12.20 p.m. the rate of fire will be Section Fire 15 seconds. The order for increased rate of fire for 10 minutes before the assult is cancelled. From 12.20 p.m. till 2.0 p.m. the rate will be as ordered in Table of rates of fire with the following exception.

5. The rate of fire of batteries shooting on HOHENZOLLERN REDOUBT and SOUTH FACE i.e. One battery 3rd Brigade on SOUTH FACE, one battery 3rd Brigade on WEST FACE and one battery 64th Brigade on points 32 33 and 1.1 and 2.4, will be maintained at Section fire 15 seconds during the whole of the first phase -(noon till 2.0 p.m.)

                                                              Major.

12th October 1915.   Brigade Major. R.A. 28th Division.

146th Bde   Copy No 3

Amendments to Operation Order No. 51 dated 9th October 1915.

Paragraph 1 -- for 12th read 13th

Paragraph 13 -- Amended distribution of fire herewith. The copy forwarded with the Operation Order should be returned.

Acknowledge

[signature]

Major

10th October 1915.   Brigade Major R.A. 28th Division

146th Bde

Copy No. 3

28th Divisional Artillery

SECRET

Operation Order No. 51.

Reference Map 1/10,000   9th October 1915.

1.   The XIth Corps will, on the 13th instant, attack and capture the QUARRIES and FOSSE No. 8.

The LINE which will be established runs from G 12 d 3.9 G 12 b 2.2 - G 6 c 8.2 and 4.5 - G 6 a 4.2 - A 29 d 2.5 N.W. corner of CORONS DE MARON A 29 c 1.6 - A 28 d 4.9 and along AUCHY - LEZ - LA - BASSEE - VERMELLES Road to present front trench A 28 c 3.3

2.   Point of junction between 46th and 12th Divisions is G 5 b 6.8

3.   28th Divisional Artillery will support the attack of the 46th Division which will be launched at 2.0 p.m.

4.   46th Division will deliver a LEFT and a RIGHT ATTACK, the dividing line between them will be G 4 b 6.0 - right edge of FOSSE COTTAGES and the PENTAGON.

5.   FIRST OBJECTIVE LEFT ATTACK.

PENTAGON (exclusive) A 29 c 1.6, A 28 d 6.3 and 4.3, to present front trench at A 28 c 5.1

6.   SECOND OBJECTIVE.

Railway A 29 c 1.6 (inclusive) A 28 d 4.9 - LAL POINT to front trench A 28 c 3.3

(7)   RIGHT ATTACK. FIRST OBJECTIVE.

TRACK crossing FOSSE ALLEY at G 5 c 6.8 - G 5 c 3.9 and 2.2 PENTAGON (inclusive)

8.   SECOND OBJECTIVE.

A 29 d 2.5, 3 Cabarets, N.L. edge of CORON de PUITS - West edge of CORONS DE MARON Railway A 29 c 1.6 (exclusive)

9.   The Preliminary bombardment will commence at 12 noon and will continue until 2.0 p.m.

(2)

H.E. will be fired up to 1.0 p.m. at which hour smoke and gas will be launched and shrapnel only will be fired for the remainder of that phase and the succeeding ones.

Separate orders have been given to 4.5" Howitzers.

10. The F.O.Officers of the 146th and 3rd Brigades now with the LEFT and RIGHT Battalions of the 2nd Guards Brigade and the F.O.Officers of the 22nd Brigade, hitherto found by the 35th Brigade now with the RIGHT and LEFT Battalions of the 1st Guards Brigade will accompany the Battalion Commanders of the assulting Battalions in the attack. The F.O.O. of the 36th brigade and of the 22nd brigade now with the 2nd and 1st Guards Brigade H.Q. will remain with Headquarters of LEFT and RIGHT attack, namely the H.Q. of the 138th and 137th brigades respectively.

11. The F.O.O. of the single gun of the 64th Brigade near WILLS will establish a visual signalling station on the dump at the first opportunity. He will also run out wires to connect him with his gun.

12. A visual signalling station will be established by the 3rd brigade near the WILLS.

13. The programme for the distribution of fire for the 28th Divisional Artillery and affiliated brigades is forwarded herewith.

14. Acknowledge.

Major,
Brigade Major R.A. 28th Division.

Copy No. 1 filed
Copy No. 2 3rd Brigade
Copy No. 3 146th Brigade
Copy No. 4 138th Brigade
Copy No. 5 36th Brigade
Copy No. 6 22nd Brigade
Copy No. 7 46th Division
Copy No. 8 XIth Corps

DISTRIBUTION OF FIRE OF 28TH DIVISIONAL ARTILLERY

First Phase.

Bombardment — Noon till 2.0 p.m.

Gas — 1.0 p.m. till 1.50 p.m.

Smoke — 1.0 p.m. till 2.0 p.m.

3rd Brigade.

- 1 battery — WEST FACE as far South as G 4 b 5.0
- 1 battery — NORTH FACE
- 1 battery — DUMP TRENCH between points 97 and 35
- 1 battery — SOUTH FACE from point 35 to G 4 b 7.2

146th Brigade.

- 1 battery — LITTLE WILLIE Northern Half
- 1 battery — LITTLE WILLIE Southern Half
- 1 battery — FOSSE TRENCH 43 - 97

22nd Brigade.

- 1 battery — ~~FOSSE TRENCH - MAD POINT~~ SLAG ALLEY not further South than G 5 a 8.4
- 1 battery — PENTAGON (A 29 c 5.3) to G 5.a 5.5

36th Brigade.

- 1 battery — FOSSE TRENCH. MAD POINT to point A 28 d 5.2
- 1 battery — A 28 d 5.2 to G 4 b 9.7
- 1 battery — Communication trenches N.E. of FOSSE TRENCH in A 28 d especially CORONS ALLEY and Trench A 28 d 4.8 to A 29 c 2.6

64th Brigade.

- 1 battery — HOLLENZOLLERN 32 - 33
- 1 battery — Trench G 5 a 5½.7 to G 5 a 1½.7½
- 1 battery — S.W. face of DUMP

Howitzers. 130th Brigade.

- 1 battery — Communication trench A 28 d 4½.2 to 8½.6) From 12 noon to 1 pm firing LYDDITE. From 1 pm to 1.45 pm LYDDITE on MAD POINT and MADAGASCAR
- 1 battery — LITTLE WILLIE Northern Half
- 1 battery — LITTLE WILLIE Southern Half — 12 noon to 1 pm. At 1 pm fire on AUCHY LA BASSEE slow rate Lyddite till 1.45 pm

28th Divisional Artillery.

Addition to Operation Order No. 51 dated 9th October 1915.

1. Distinguishing flags.

    Infantry will carry 3 foot square screens divided diagonally into red and yellow to mark the position of the firing line.

    Bombing parties will mark their positions in captured trenches by red flags 18 inches square.

2. Acknowledge.

[signature]

Major.

11th October 1915.   Brigade Major R.A. 28th Division.

Batteries informed
[initials]

2nd Divn, Bombers yellow

SECRET

146ᵗʰ Bde.

1ˢᵗ ½ hr × fᵐ 15 secs
also ¼ hr ? assault

B.M. 532
11th October 1915.

The following table shows, rates of fire to be employed in carrying out the programme on the 13th instant.

1. **18-pounder batteries.**

240   60   From 12 noon to 1.0 p.m.   Section fire 30 seconds
 60   30 -   1.0 p.m. to 2.0 p.m.   ..   .. 2 minutes
160 185 50 -   2.0 p.m. to 4.0 p.m.   ..   .. 1½ minutes
 90   45ˣ   4.0 p.m. to 5.30 p.m.   ..   .. 2 minutes
 55

ˣ During this period equal proportions of H.E. and Shrapnel will be used.

2. **4.5" (Howitzer) Batteries.**

A.B. & C.   From 12 noon to 1.45 pm   Section fire 1 minute
A & B (Lachry-) 1.45 pm to 2.30 pm   ..   .. 1 minute
      (matory)
  C   (shell) 1.45 pm to 2.0 pm   ..   .. 15 seconds
A and B   2.30 pm to 5.30 pm)
)   ..   .. 1 minute
  C   2.0 pm to 5.30 pm   )

3.   In the event of the wind being unfavourable and the gas not being employed the amount of ammunition to be expended - as authorised in above table - will be increased by 20% of the whole amount during the first two hours. Under present arrangements 18-pounders will fire 200 rounds per gun, and 4.5" Howitzers 150 rounds per Howitzer exclusive of Lachrymatory shell.

M. Ferguson
                                             Major.
                           Brigade Major R.A. 28th Division.

120
180
 90
120
160
160
850

S E C R E T.   Copy No. 9

28th Divisional Artillery
Operation Order No. 52.

                                                16th October 1915.

Reference Map. Trench Map 1/50,000

1. At 5.0 a.m. tomorrow, the 17th instant, the 2nd and 3rd Guards Brigades will commence bombing operations with a view of driving the enemy from BIG WILLIE and joining hands across it.

The 3rd Brigade will also try to bomb up DUMP TRENCH sufficiently far to cut off SOUTH FACE.

2. The Heavy Artillery will co-operate by bombarding undermentioned points at the rate of 6 rounds per hour for the H.A.R. and 8 rounds an hour for the Seige Group.

    5th H.A.R.   FOSSE TRENCH
                  FOSSE Support Trench
                  MAD POINT
                  MADAGASCAR
                  PENTAGON.

    Seige Group. COHON'S ALLEY from 1.6 to 9.0
                 SLAG ALLEY
                 FRONT ROW FOSSE COTTAGES

3. The programme for the distribution of the fire of the 28th Divisional Artillery is attached.

4. In future, when practicable, the progress of a bombing attack will be shewn by the waving of a signalling flag at short intervals of time, about 50 yards behind the front of the attack. It is considered that no more conspicuous signal than this is either practicable or desirable.

5. Fire on the allotted points will commence at 5.0 a.m. Rate of fire section fire 30 seconds for 18-pdrs, and 2 minutes for Howitzers.

6. Acknowledge.

                                    M Fergusson
                                            Major,
                             Brigade Major R.A. 28th Division.

Copy No. 1   Filed
Copy No. 2   Guards Divn.
Copy No. 3   XIth Corps
Copy No. 4   3rd Bde.
Copy No. 5   22nd Bde.
Copy No. 6   36th Bde.
Copy No. 7   64th Bde.
Copy No. 8   130th Bde.
Copy No. 9   146th Bde.

7 50 pm

Programme of the distribution of fire to support the Bombing attack of the Guards brigades.

----

1. **3rd brigade.**

    1 battery   NORTH FACE especially point 97
    1 battery   Trench G 5 a 1½.8 to 5.7 especially points 1½.8 and 5.7
    1 battery   Trench 90.97 especially points 90 and 97
    1 battery   DUMP TRENCH 97 to 17 and Trench 9½ 9 to 17 especially points 9½ 9 and 1 7

2. **22nd brigade.**

    2 batteries   PENTAGON and Trench to South to point 57 especially PENTAGON and point 5.7
    1 battery   SLAG ALLEY especially point 39
    1 gun   SLAG ALLEY

3. **36th brigade.**

    1 battery   MAD POINT to point 15 especially point 15
    1 battery   FOSSE TRENCH 15 to 43 especially points 2½.3½, 43
    1 battery   Support and Communication Trenches 3.6⅞ to 4½.4⅞ and 15 to 16. Especially points 36½.86

4. **64th brigade.**

    1 battery   Trench G 5 a 1½.8 to 5.7 especially points 1½.8 and 5.7
    2 batteries COROFS ALLEY especially points 16 and 90

5. **146th brigade.**

    149. 1 battery   FOSSE TRENCH 43.61 especially points 4⅞.2 5½ 4
    75   1 battery   FOSSE TRENCH 61.97 especially points 61.89
    367. 1 battery   Support and Communication trench behind this especially points 5½.4 and 6.2

6. **150th (Howitzer) brigade.**

    1 battery   A 28 d 9.0 and trenches about front two rows of FOSSE COTTAGES.
    1 battery   PENTAGON
    1 battery   N.E. of the DUMP along road and railway line as far South as SLAG ALLEY.

SECRET.

146 R Bde RFA

Copy No.

28th Divisional Artillery Operation Order No. 53.

18th October 1915.

1. The first sections of 28th Divisional Artillery will be relieved by the first sections of Guards Divisional Artillery by 6.30 p.m on the night 19th/20th, and will, in their turn, relieve first sections of the Meerut Divisional Artillery on the night 20th/21st, with the exception of 3rd Brigade and one battery, 130th Brigade.

2. Remaining sections will be relieved by 6.30 p.m. on night 20th/21st, and will take over from Meerut Divisional Artillery on night 21st/22nd. C.R.A. 28th Division will assume command of batteries covering the new front at 10 a.m. 21st October.

3. Brigade Commanders of 31st, 146th and 130th Brigades will assume command of their new positions at 10 a.m. on the 22nd.

4. Brigades will take over positions according to attached table. The 3rd Brigade and one Howitzer Battery will proceed to rest area, which will be notified later.

5. Sections, on the night they are relieved, will proceed to their wagon lines.

6. Acknowledge.

Major

Issued 11 p.m.   Brigade Major, Royal Artillery, 28th Divn.

Copy No. 1. Filed.
 ,, 2. 3rd Brigade, RFA
 ,, 3. 31st ,,
 ,, 4. 146th ,,
 ,, 5. 130th ,,
 ,, 6. 12th Divl. Arty.
 ,, 7. 2nd ,,
 ,, 8. Meerut ,,
 ,, 9. 1st Corps Arty.
 ,, 10. 11th ,,
 ,, 11. 28th Division

www.ingramcontent.com/pod-product-compliance
Lightning Source LLC
Chambersburg PA
CBHW081428160426
43193CB00013B/2220